絶対『英語の耳』になる！TVドラマ・シーンで鍛える！

ネイティヴ英語リスニング37

長尾和夫＋アンディ・バーガー●著

三修社

Preface
はじめに

　本書は、英語を学習しようとしている多くの方の目標のひとつでもある**「ドラマの英語の聴き取り」を鍛える**ために、『絶対「英語の耳」になる!』シリーズの 12 作目の書籍として企画されたものです。

　「英語の音声だけでドラマが理解できたら」と思ってはいても、ドラマの中に登場するボキャブラリーや、ネイティヴたちの早口に入り交じった音声変化の極端さになかなかついていけず、仕方なく字幕や吹き替えを選択しているというのが、多くの学習者のみなさんの実情ではないでしょうか。

　また、**ドラマには多様なジャンルがあって、それぞれに独特のボキャブラリーが含まれている**のも、リスニングを難しくしている一因です。
　本書では、少しでもドラマの英語に近づきたい方を読者層として想定し、多様なジャンルのドラマの典型的なシーンを 37 本用意しました。オリジナルのダイアローグでは、**ジャンルごとに、可能な限り典型的な言い回しやストーリー展開を組み込む工夫を凝らし、まさに実際のドラマに登場しそうなシーンを数多く掲載**することができたと考えています。

　例えば、ギャング・ドラマのユニットの第一声は次のようになっています。

> **Carlo, it's time for you to come clean. You can't bullshit your way out of this.**
> (カルロ、白状する時間だ。お前は、この件をごまかすことなんてできないんだよ)

　ここで登場する come clean「白状する」、bullshit「だます ; ほらを吹く ; うそをつく」などはギャング・ドラマには典型的なボキャブラリーに属するものです。
　ネイティヴはもちろんこういった独特の言い回しやスラングなどを自然に身につけていますが、これらの**ちょっとした語彙がわからないだけでも、リスニングの際には大変な混乱が生じる**ものです。さらに、ドラマの中のネイティヴたちの英会話スピードは教科書や一般の英会話書籍よりもさらに早口な場合が多いため、英語学習の中・

上級レベルの人であっても、かなりハードルが高いものなのです。

　これはシリーズの前作『絶対「英語音の耳」になる！ 37のインタビューで鍛える！ ネイティヴ英語リスニング』にも言えることですが、ドラマの英語では、**話し手＝役者の感情の揺れによって、トーンやスピード、抑揚などがさらに強く変化する**ため、聴き取りがいっそう難しくなります。このように、「ドラマの英語」の中には、**英語の聴き取りを最大限に困難にする要素が大量かつ濃厚に含まれている**のです。

　本書に用意した37のオリジナルのドラマ・シーンには、すでにご紹介した**ギャング・ドラマのほか、ラブコメ、青春ドラマ、探偵ドラマ、セクシー・ミステリー、業界ドラマ、法律ドラマ、歴史ドラマ、ゴースト・ドラマなど、多種多様なジャンル**を用意しました。
　吹き込みには、プロの俳優、ナレーターに参加してもらい、臨場感豊かなCDを実現できたと思います。CD音声はナチュラル・スピードのほかに、ナチュラルよりもややゆっくり目のスロー（スロー・ナチュラル）スピードの音声も加えてありますから、**自分のレベルに合わせて音声を選択しながら学習**を進めていただくことも可能です。

　さあ、みなさんも「ドラマの英語を聴き取る特訓」を本書で行ってください。多様なキャラクターのさまざまな感情の抑揚、語り口がみなさんの耳に飛び込んできます。もちろん、本書は、テレビ・ドラマだけではなく、映画英語の聴き取りにも同様の効果を発揮してくれるはずです。
　本書を通じて、「ドラマ英語の実際」を学んだみなさんの、聴き取り能力が向上し、英語のテレビ・ドラマや映画の観賞がさらに楽しみな時間になったとしたら、著者としてこれ以上のよろこびはありません。

　最後になりますが、本書の刊行にご尽力いただいた三修社のスタッフのみなさんに、心からの感謝を申し上げます。

A+Café 代表 長尾和夫
2015年4月1日

Contents
もくじ

Preface はじめに 2
How to Use 本書の使い方 6
本書に登場する「ルールの用語」と「記号」...... 8

Unit 1 シングル女性ドラマ
Single Women's Drama (Sex and the City type) 10

Unit 2 ギャング・ドラマ
Gangster Drama (The Sopranos type) 16

Unit 3 シングル・コメディー
Singles Comedy (Friends type) 22

Unit 4 ホスピタル・ドラマ
Hospital Drama (ER type) 28

Unit 5 政治ドラマ
Political Drama (West Wing type) 34

Unit 6 SFドラマ
Sci-Fi Drama (Star Trek type) 40

Unit 7 法律コメディー
Legal Comedy (Ally McBeal type) 46

Unit 8 対テロリスト・ドラマ
Hostage/Terrorist Drama (24 type) 52

Unit 9 超自然ドラマ
Supernatural Drama (Lost type) 58

Unit 10 オフィス・コメディー
Workplace Comedy (Ugly Betty type) 64

Unit 11 逃亡者ドラマ
Escapee Drama (Prison Break type) 70

Unit 12 青春ドラマ
Teenager Drama (Glee type) 76

Unit 13 警察ドラマ
Police Drama (Cops type) 82

Unit 14 高校生ドラマ
High School Drama (Beverly Hills 90210 type) 88

Unit 15 ファミリー・コメディー
Family Comedy (Full House type) 94

Unit 16 歴史ドラマ
Ancient Times Drama (Game of Thrones type) 100

Unit 17 探偵ドラマ
Detective Drama (Sherlock type) 106

Unit 18 ゾンビ・ドラマ
Zombie Drama (Walking Dead type) 112

Unit 19 ヴァンパイア・ドラマ
Vampire Drama (Twilight type) 118

Unit 20 ファミリー・ドラマ
Family Drama (Heartland type) 124

Unit 21 ゴースト・ドラマ
Ghost Drama (Supernatural type) 130

Unit 22 オタク・コメディー
Geek Comedy (Big Bang Theory type) 136

Unit 23 ラブコメ
Romance Comedy (How I Met Your Mother type) 142

Unit 24 セクシー・ミステリー・ドラマ
Sex/Mystery Drama (Desperate Housewives type) 148

Unit 25 犯罪ドラマ
Crime Drama (Breaking Bad type) 154

Unit 26 広告業界ドラマ
Advertising Industry Drama (Mad Men type) 160

Unit 27 超常現象ドラマ
Paranormal Drama (X-Files type) 166

Unit 28 スーパーヒーロー・ドラマ
Superhero Drama (Smallville type) 172

Unit 29 企業コメディー
Corporate Comedy (The Office type) 178

Unit 30 独身男性コメディー
Bachelor Comedy (Two and a Half Men type) 184

Unit 31 スポーツ・コメディー
Sports Comedy (Anger Management type) 190

Unit 32 バー・コメディー
Bar Comedy (Cheers type) 196

Unit 33 犯罪捜査ドラマ
Crime Investigation Drama (CSI type) 202

Unit 34 戦争ドラマ
War Drama (Band of Brothers type) 208

Unit 35 医療系ラブコメ
Doctor/Romance Comedy (Grey's Anatomy type) 214

Unit 36 エンタメ業界ドラマ
Entertainment Industry Drama (30 Rock type) 220

Unit 37 法律ドラマ
Legal Drama (Law & Order type) 226

How to Use 本書の使い方

Ⓐ ドラマ・シーンの通し番号とドラマ・シーンの見出し
　ドラマ・シーンの番号と見出しを掲載してあります。見出しを見れば、どのような内容やタイプのドラマかがわかります。また、見出しの後ろの（　）の中には、既存のドラマではどのドラマのタイプに分類できるかを記載しておきました。

Ⓑ Stage1：穴埋めドラマ・リスニング
　まず最初のステージでは、CDを聴きながら空欄部分を穴埋めしてみましょう。空欄部分には音声変化を含む英単語や英語のフレーズが入ります。注意して聴き取りすべての空欄に、聴き取れたフレーズを記入しましょう。
　CDには、各ドラマ・シーンの音声が2種類収録されています。ユニットの音声を再生すると、最初に聴こえてくるのがナチュラル・スピードのドラマ・シーン音声、さらに次のトラックに収録されているのがスロー・スピード（ナチュラルよりやや遅いスピード）の音声です。
　まず最初は、ナチュラル・スピードの音声で穴埋めを行い、どうしても聴き取れなかった場合は、スロー・スピードの音声で聴き直してみてもいいでしょう。
　ただし、スロー音声はあくまでも最初のステップとし、最終的にはナチュラル・スピードでドラマ・シーンが聴き取れるようになるまでトレーニングを行ってください。

Ⓒ 空欄つきドラマ・シーン原稿
　①～⑮の番号の後ろの空欄を穴埋めしてみましょう。

Ⓓ Stage2：ドラマのシーン解説
　ここでは、Stage 1のドラマ・シーンで登場した語句と日本語訳をチェック、理解していきましょう。ドラマに頻出の独特な英単語やフレーズの解説とドラマ・シーンの日本語訳を、該当する英文のブロッ

クのすぐ下に、簡潔にまとめておきました。
　解説や日本語訳で内容をしっかり理解したら、もう一度 Stage 1 に立ち戻って音声を聴き直してみましょう。語句や表現を知っている場合と知らない場合に、どのようにリスニング力が異なるか強く実感できると思います。

E Stage3：英文トランスクリプション
　Stage 3 はインタビューの英文だけをすべて文字に起こし、読みやすいよう 1 ページにまとめて書き出してあります。穴埋めできていなかったところを太字部分でチェックしてみてから、もう一度ドラマ・シーンの音声を聴き取ってみましょう。さらに格段に英文がよく聴き取れるのが実感できるはずです。

F Stage4：音声変化をチェック
　Stage 4 は、ドラマ・シーンのリスニングのまとめとして、空欄部分の音声を、変化していないスロー・スピード音声と変化後のナチュラル・スピード音声の両方で収録してあります。
　テキストでは、左から順に
【英語の語句】－【変化前の音声のカタカナ表記】－【変化後の音声のカタカナ表記】
　の順で示してあります。また、次の行では ☞ マークのあとに**【音声変化のルール】**を、わかりやすい表現で簡潔に解説しておきました。
　このステージで、音声変化にさらに耳慣らししてから、最後にもう一度ドラマ・シーンの英語の聴き取りにチャレンジしてみましょう。

　学習の順番はみなさんの考えで変更していただいてもいいでしょう。本書の狙いはあくまでもボキャブラリーと音声変化の法則を身につけながらドラマ・シーンの英語に耳慣らししていくことなのです。その点だけをしっかり頭に入れて学習を進めてください。
　また、CD 音声は、書籍といっしょに用いる以外にも、音声だけを携帯音楽プレーヤーなどに保存し、日々の空き時間などを利用して聴き取り練習を行ってみましょう。ドラマ・シーンの音声を 2 種類用意したのは、学習者のレベルに対応するためでもありますが、さらにスロー・スピードとナチュラル・スピードの音声を聴き比べしながら、ネイティヴ英語の音声変化に、毎日のように親しんでいただきたかったからです。
　では、学習をスタートしましょう！

本書に登場する「ルールの用語」と「記号」

本書では発音のルールを説明するために、次の6つの用語と記号をおもに用いています。本文の音声CD音声を聴きながら、以下の用語を実地で確認していきましょう。

❶ **脱落**：英語の音の一部が消えてなくなる場合に「脱落」という言葉で説明しています。例えば、good boy の good では [d] の音が脱落してなくなり、「グッ＿ボーイ」のように発話される傾向にあります。

❷ **連結**：英語の音声の中で子音と母音が連続する場面では、音の連結が頻繁に生じます。リエゾンとも呼ばれます。例えば、on it「オン・イット」の [n] の音に it の [ɪ] の音が連なって「オニット」といった発音に変化しますが、これを連結として説明しています。

❸ **弾音化**：英語の破裂音 [t] や [d] などに母音が連なっているところで、よくこの弾音化が起こります。例えば、get away では、get の [t] に away の先頭の母音 [ə] が連なっていますが、この [tə] の部分が［タ］ではなく［ダ］や［ラ］に近い弾くような音に変化してしまいます。「ゲッタウェイ」ではなく「ゲッダ［ラ］ウェイ」のように聴こえるとき、これを弾音化していると言います。

❹ **同化**：同化とは、2つの音が混じり合って、元の音とは別の音になってしまうことです。例えば、meet you では、meet 末尾の [t] の音と you の頭の [j] が混じり合って別の「チュ」といった音に変化します。

❺ **声門閉鎖音化**：声門閉鎖音化とは、button のような単語で [tn] が連続する場面などで生じます。この場合、[t] の音が変化して「バトゥン」ではなく、「バンン」のように聴こえる発音になります。このとき、喉の声門が咳払いをする直前のような状態で閉じられているため、この音声変化を声門閉鎖音化と呼んでいます。

❻ **記号**：本書では発音変化をカタカナ表記していますが、その中で次の記号を使用しています。
　［　］ブラケットは直前の音と入れ換え可能という意味で用いています。
　（　）丸括弧は、囲まれている音が脱落する場合があることを示しています。
　＿　アンダーバーは、その部分の音声が脱落することを示しています。

絶対『英語の耳』になる！
TVドラマ・シーンで鍛える！
ネイティヴ英語リスニング37

Your New English Ears
37 Typical Dialogs from TV Dramas

Unit 1 シングル女性ドラマ

Single Women's Drama (Sex and the City type)

Stage 1 穴埋めドラマ・リスニング

音声変化に注意してCDでドラマの音声を聴きながら空欄部分を埋めてみよう。CDのナチュラル音声での聴き取りが難しいときは、次のトラックに収録されたスロー音声で聴いてみよう。

● ● ● ● ● ●

A This is a rare treat! Drinks in the afternoon? We ① _____ _____ this since, like, our college days, have we?

B It's uh, strategic. Believe me, girlfriend, we both are ② _____ _____ need these.

A Huh? ③ _____ _____ _____ mean?

B Me, so I can have the courage to ④ _____ _____ out. You, for when you hear it.

A Yikes! That bad, huh? All right, I'm ready. You can spill the beans.

B Sarah, I saw Jake last night. Just on the street. I'm ⑤ _____ sure he ⑥ _____ see me. ⑦ _____ _____ was, oh god, he was with Rebecca.

A That's it? That's ⑧ _____ _____ needed these drinks for? You silly! Jake and Rebecca are old friends.

B No, look, Sarah ... they weren't ⑨ _____ ... well, let's say they weren't ACTING like friends.

10

A Uh oh. I think I need another drink. ⑩ _____!

B Oh, honey, I'm so sorry to have to be the one ⑪ _____ tell you.

A So, ⑫ _____ _____ you saying, ⑬ _____? Were they, what? All touchy-feely? Kissing? Were tongues involved? What?

B Um ... all of the above?

A Oh! How ⑭ _____ _____ do this to me? Both of them! I feel like I ⑮ _____ kill them both!

Stage 2 ドラマのシーン解説

日本語訳と、解説を参照しながら、ドラマの内容を確認しよう。そのあとで、Stage1の穴埋めに再チャレンジしてみよう。

A This is a rare treat! Drinks in the afternoon? We ① **haven't done** this since, like, our college days, have we?

すごく貴重なごちそうね！ 午後にお酒？ こういうの、なんだか学生時代以来よね？

＊ rare「稀な；貴重な」

B It's uh, strategic. Believe me, girlfriend, we both are ② **going to** need these.

ああ、言わば、これは戦略なのよ。友よ、信じて、私たちにはこれが必要になるのよ。

＊ strategic「戦略的な；戦略に基づく」

シングル女性ドラマ 11

A Huh? ③ **What do you** mean?

え？　どういう意味？

B Me, so I can have the courage to ④ **get this** out. You, for when you hear it.

私にとっては、これを告白する勇気が要るし、あなたはそれを聞くために必要なのよ。

＊ get out「(努力して) 口に出す」

A Yikes! That bad, huh? All right, I'm ready. You can spill the beans.

ええっ！　そんなにヤバイこと？　いいわ、心の準備はできたから。話して。

＊ Yikes.「うわっ；ゲッ」驚きや嫌悪を表す。　spill the beans「秘密などを漏らす」

B Sarah, I saw Jake last night. Just on the street. I'm ⑤ **pretty** sure he ⑥ **didn't** see me. ⑦ **But he** was, oh god, he was with Rebecca.

サラ、私ね、昨日の夜、ジェイクを見たの。通りでね。きっと彼、私のことは見てなかったと思うわ。でも、彼ね、ああ神様、彼はレベッカといっしょだったの。

A That's it? That's ⑧ **what we** needed these drinks for? You silly! Jake and Rebecca are old friends.

それだけ？　で、このお酒が必要だったわけ？　どうかしてるわよ！　ジェイクとレベッカは古い友達じゃない。

＊ silly「バカげた」

B No, look, Sarah ... they weren't ⑨ **exactly** ... well, let's say they weren't ACTING like friends.

いいえ、聞いてよ、サラ…ふたりは必ずしも…あのね、うーん、友達って感じで振る舞ってはいなかったの。

＊ not exactly ...「必ずしも…ない」

A Uh oh. I think I need another drink. ⑩ **Waiter**!

えっ。もう１杯お酒がいるわよね。ウェイター！

B Oh, honey, I'm so sorry to have to be the one ⑪ **to** tell you.

ああ、ハニー、私があなたにこんな話をしなきゃならないなんて。

＊ the one to tell you「あなたに話す人物」

A So, ⑫ **what are** you saying, ⑬ **exactly**? Were they, what? All touchy-feely? Kissing? Were tongues involved? What?

で、正確にはなにを言ってるのよ？ ふたりがなんだったのよ？ ベタベタしてたの？ キス？ ディープ・キスだったの？ なんなのよ？

＊ exactly「正確には」 touchy-feely「公然とベタベタして」

B Um ... all of the above?

うーん、いま言ったこと全部かなぁ…

＊ all of the above「これまでに言及されたこと全部」

A Oh! How ⑭ **could they** do this to me? Both of them! I feel like I ⑮ **could** kill them both!

ああ！ どうして私にそんなことができるのよ？ あのふたりが？ 私、ふたりを殺しちゃいそうよ！

＊ feel like ...「…みたいな気持ちだ」

シングル女性ドラマ　13

Stage 3　英文トランスクリプション

ドラマのシーン全体を英文の原稿で確認しながらCDで耳慣らししよう！ その上で、ドラマ・シーンの音声を聴きながら、まだできていない部分の穴埋めに再チャレンジしよう。

● ● ● ● ● ●

A This is a rare treat! Drinks in the afternoon? We ① **haven't done** this since, like, our college days, have we?

B It's uh, strategic. Believe me, girlfriend, we both are ② **going to** need these.

A Huh? ③ **What do you** mean?

B Me, so I can have the courage to ④ **get this** out. You, for when you hear it.

A Yikes! That bad, huh? All right, I'm ready. You can spill the beans.

B Sarah, I saw Jake last night. Just on the street. I'm ⑤ **pretty** sure he ⑥ **didn't** see me. ⑦ **But he** was, oh god, he was with Rebecca.

A That's it? That's ⑧ **what we** needed these drinks for? You silly! Jake and Rebecca are old friends.

B No, look, Sarah ... they weren't ⑨ **exactly** ... well, let's say they weren't ACTING like friends.

A Uh oh. I think I need another drink. ⑩ **Waiter**!

B Oh, honey, I'm so sorry to have to be the one ⑪ **to** tell you.

A So, ⑫ **what are** you saying, ⑬ **exactly**? Were they, what? All touchy-feely? Kissing? Were tongues involved? What?

B Um ... all of the above?

A Oh! How ⑭ **could they** do this to me? Both of them! I feel like I ⑮ **could** kill them both!

Stage 4 音声変化をチェック

まとめとして、穴埋め部分の音声変化の特徴を**スロー・スピード**と**ナチュラル・スピード**で確認しよう。下記に示したカタカナ表記で音声変化を確認して、もう一度ドラマを聴き直してみよう。発音変化のルールは適宜復習しよう。

❶ **haven't done** ハヴント・ダン ▶ ハヴン＿ダン
☞ haven't の破裂音 [t] が脱落する。

❷ **going to** ゴウイング・トゥー ▶ ゴウイン＿トゥー
☞ going の破裂音 [g] が脱落する。

❸ **What do you** ワット・ドゥー・ユー ▶ ワッ＿ドゥユ
☞ What の破裂音 [t] が脱落する。do you は弱化して [ドゥユ] と弱く短く発音される。

❹ **get this** ゲット・ズィス ▶ ゲッ＿ズィス
☞ get の破裂音 [t] が脱落する。

❺ **pretty** プリティー ▶ プリディ [リ] ー
☞ 破裂音 [t] が弾音化する。

❻ **didn't** ディドゥント ▶ ディドゥン＿
☞ 末尾の破裂音 [t] が脱落する。

❼ **But he** バット・ヒー ▶ バッ＿ヒー
☞ But の破裂音 [t] が脱落する。

❽ **what we** ワット・ウィ ▶ ワッ＿ウィ
☞ what の破裂音 [t] が脱落する。

❾ **exactly** イグザクトゥリー ▶ イグザック＿リー
☞ [tl] から、破裂音 [t] が脱落する。

❿ **Waiter** ウェイター ▶ ウェイダ [ラ] ー
☞ 破裂音 [t] が弾音化する。

⓫ **to** トゥー ▶ ドゥ [ル] ー
☞ to の破裂音 [t] が弾音化する。

⓬ **what are** ワット・アー ▶ ワッダ [ラ] ー
☞ 連結部で破裂音 [t] が弾音化する。

⓭ **exactly** イグザクトゥリー ▶ イグザック＿リー
☞ ❾ と同様の変化が起こる。

⓮ **could they** クッド・ゼイ ▶ クッ＿ゼイ
☞ could の破裂音 [d] が脱落する。

⓯ **could** クッド ▶ クッ＿
☞ 破裂音 [d] が脱落する。

Unit 2 ギャング・ドラマ
Gangster Drama (The Sopranos type)

Stage 1 穴埋めドラマ・リスニング

音声変化に注意してCDでドラマの音声を聴きながら空欄部分を埋めてみよう。CDのナチュラル音声での聴き取りが難しいときは、次のトラックに収録されたスロー音声で聴いてみよう。

● ● ● ● ●

A Carlo, it's time for you ① _____ come clean. You can't bullshit your way ② _____ _____ this.

B Sal, I swear, I don't have the slightest idea ③ _____ _____ talking about.

A That's not the way to play this, Carlo. ④ _____ _____ _____ give you one last chance to spill the beans.

B What? ⑤ _____ _____ talked to Frankie Pacino? You had me tagged?

A You're still ⑥ _____ _____ try to lie, huh? You ⑦ _____ just 'talk' to Pacino. You made a deal.

B No, I ⑧ _____! I swear, Sal, on my mother's soul! I would never go ⑨ _____ _____ back.

A That's exactly ⑩ _____ _____ did, you slimy backstabber! You ⑪ _____ _____ set me up.

B No, no, Sal! You ⑫ _____ _____ all wrong! I don't know

16

what you heard, but ...

A You really think I'm stupid, huh? Too old to notice when someone in my organization is ⑬ _____ _____ whack me?

B Sal, no! I'm your right hand man! I would never ...

A So long, Carlo. Just so you know, Pacino ⑭ _____ _____ _____ _____ ago. I just ⑮ _____ _____ call.

B Oh, god, NO! Sal, PLEASE ...!

< Bang Bang Bang!!!! >

Stage 2 ドラマのシーン解説

日本語訳と、解説を参照しながら、ドラマの内容を確認しよう。そのあとで、Stage1の穴埋めに再チャレンジしてみよう。

A Carlo, it's time for you ① **to** come clean. You can't bullshit your way ② **out of** this.

カルロ、白状する時間だ。お前は、この件をごまかすことなんてできないんだよ。

＊ come clean「白状する」 bullshit「だます；ほらを吹く；うそをつく」

B Sal, I swear, I don't have the slightest idea ③ **what you're** talking about.

サル、誓うよ。あんたがなにを言ってるかさっぱりわからないんだ。

＊ slightest = slight「わずかな」の最上級。

A That's not the way to play this, Carlo. ④ **I'm going to** give you one last chance to spill the beans.

遊びじゃないんだよ、これは、カルロ。最後のチャンスをやるから、白状しろ。

* spill the beans「秘密などをバラす；白状する」

B What? ⑤ **That I** talked to Frankie Pacino? You had me tagged?

え？ 俺がフランキー・パチーノと話したってことか？ 俺を尾行させたってのかい？

* have someone tagged「…を尾行させる」

A You're still ⑥ **going to** try to lie, huh? You ⑦ **didn't** just 'talk' to Pacino. You made a deal.

まだ俺をだまそうとしているのか、あー？ お前は、パチーノと単に話をしただけじゃない。取引したんだよ。

* make a deal「取引する」

B No, I ⑧ **didn't**! I swear, Sal, on my mother's soul! I would never go ⑨ **behind your** back.

やってない！ サル、母親の魂に誓って！ あんたを決して裏切ったりはしないよ。

* go behind someone's back「…に背く；裏切る」

A That's exactly ⑩ **what you** did, you slimy backstabber! You ⑪ **tried to** set me up.

それこそ、お前がやったことだ。このいやらしい裏切り者が！ お前は、俺をはめようとしたんだよ。

* slimy「いやらしい；不快な」 backstabber「陰で中傷する者；裏切り者」 set ... up「…をはめる」

B No, no, Sal! You ⑫ **got it** all wrong! I don't know what you heard, but ...

違う、違うんだ、サル！ あんたは勘違いしてるんだ！ あんたが、なにを聞いたのかは知らないが…

* get it all wrong「すっかりそれを取り違っている」

A You really think I'm stupid, huh? Too old to notice when someone in my organization is ⑬ **out to** whack me?

ホントに俺をマヌケだと思っているのか、あー？ 自分の組織のだれかが俺を殺ろうとしてるときに、気づかないほどぼけてるとでも？

* organization「組織」　whack「殺す；暗殺する」

B Sal, no! I'm your right hand man! I would never ...

サル、違うんだ！ 俺はあんたの右腕じゃないか！ 俺は決して…

A So long, Carlo. Just so you know, Pacino ⑭ **bought it an hour** ago. I just ⑮ **got the** call.

あばよ、カルロ。伝えておくが、パチーノは１時間前にあの世へ行ったよ。さっき電話をもらってな。

* buy it「死ぬ；あの世へ行く」

B Oh, god, NO! Sal, PLEASE ...!

ああ、神さま、違うんだ！ サル、お願だ…！

< Bang Bang Bang!!!! >

パーン・パン・パーン！！！（銃声）

Stage 3 英文トランスクリプション

ドラマのシーン全体を英文の原稿で確認しながらCDで耳慣らししよう！ その上で、ドラマ・シーンの音声を聴きながら、まだできていない部分の穴埋めに再チャレンジしよう。

● ● ● ● ● ●

A Carlo, it's time for you ① **to** come clean. You can't bullshit your way ② **out of** this.

B Sal, I swear, I don't have the slightest idea ③ **what you're** talking about.

A That's not the way to play this, Carlo. ④ **I'm going to** give you one last chance to spill the beans.

B What? ⑤ **That I** talked to Frankie Pacino? You had me tagged?

A You're still ⑥ **going to** try to lie, huh? You ⑦ **didn't** just 'talk' to Pacino. You made a deal.

B No, I ⑧ **didn't**! I swear, Sal, on my mother's soul! I would never go ⑨ **behind your** back.

A That's exactly ⑩ **what you** did, you slimy backstabber! You ⑪ **tried to** set me up.

B No, no, Sal! You ⑫ **got it** all wrong! I don't know what you heard, but ...

A You really think I'm stupid, huh? Too old to notice when someone in my organization is ⑬ **out to** whack me?

B Sal, no! I'm your right hand man! I would never ...

A So long, Carlo. Just so you know, Pacino ⑭ **bought it an hour** ago. I just ⑮ **got the** call.

B Oh, god, NO! Sal, PLEASE ...!

< Bang Bang Bang!!!! >

Stage 4 音声変化をチェック

まとめとして、穴埋め部分の音声変化の特徴を**スロー・スピード**と**ナチュラル・スピード**で確認しよう。下記に示したカタカナ表記で音声変化を確認して、もう一度ドラマを聴き直してみよう。発音変化のルールは適宜復習しよう。

❶ to 　　　　　　　　　　トゥー　　　　　　　　　▶ ドゥ[ル] ー
☞ 破裂音 [t] が弾音化する。

❷ out of 　　　　　　　　アウト・ァヴ　　　　　　　▶ アウダ[ラ]＿
☞ 連結部で破裂音 [t] が弾音化する。of 末尾の [v] 音は脱落。

❸ what you're 　　　　　　ワット・ユーアー　　　　　▶ ワッチュア
☞ [t] + [j] の部分で音が混じり合い、[チュ] に近い音に変化する。

❹ I'm going to 　　　　　アイム・ゴウイング・トゥー　▶ アイムゴナ
☞ going to が [ゴナ] と大きく変化する。

❺ That I 　　　　　　　　ザット・アイ　　　　　　　▶ ザッダ[ラ] イ
☞ 連結部で破裂音 [t] が弾音化する。

❻ going to 　　　　　　　ゴウイング・トゥー　　　　▶ ゴナ
☞ ❹ と同様の変化が生じる。

❼ didn't 　　　　　　　　ディドゥント　　　　　　　▶ ディドゥン＿
☞ 末尾の破裂音 [t] が脱落する。

❽ didn't 　　　　　　　　ディドゥント　　　　　　　▶ ディんント
☞ [dn] の [d] 音が声門閉鎖音化する。

❾ behind your 　　　　　ビハインド・ユア　　　　　▶ ビハインジュア
☞ [d] + [j] の部分で音が混じり合い、[ジュ] に近い音に変化する。

❿ what you 　　　　　　　ワット・ユー　　　　　　　▶ ワッチュー
☞ [t] + [j] の部分で音が混じり合い、[チュ] に近い音に変化する。

⓫ tried to 　　　　　　　トゥライド・トゥー　　　　▶ チュライッ＿ドゥ[ル] ー＿
☞ [tr] 部分の [t] 音が [チュ] に近い音に変化する。tried 末尾の [d] 音が脱落。to では [t] 音の弾音化が起こる。

⓬ got it 　　　　　　　　ガット・イット　　　　　　▶ ガッディ[リ] ッ＿
☞ 連結部で破裂音 [t] が弾音化する。it 末尾の [t] 音は脱落。

⓭ out to 　　　　　　　　アウト・トゥー　　　　　　▶ アウッ＿トゥー
☞ out の破裂音 [t] が脱落する。

⓮ bought it an hour 　ボート・イット・アン・アワー ▶ ボーディ[リ] ッダ[ラ] ナワー
☞ 4 語が連結。bought it an の連結部 2 カ所で破裂音 [t] が弾音化する。

⓯ got the 　　　　　　　ゴット・ザ　　　　　　　　▶ ゴッ＿ザ
☞ 破裂音 [t] が脱落する。

ギャング・ドラマ

Unit 3

シングル・コメディー

Singles Comedy (Friends type)

Stage 1 穴埋めドラマ・リスニング

音声変化に注意してCDでドラマの音声を聴きながら空欄部分を埋めてみよう。CDのナチュラル音声での聴き取りが難しいときは、次のトラックに収録されたスロー音声で聴いてみよう。

● ● ● ● ●

A Karen, is there any way I can ① _____ _____ _____ the friend zone with you?

B Oh, Carl! You're so funny!

A I guess that ... ② _____ _____ answers my question, huh?

B ③ _____ _____ minute. You're not serious, are you?

A I am. I mean, I was. I mean, I ④ _____ YOU ⑤ _____ think I was being serious.

B Carl! ⑥ _____ _____ _____ have known each other since we were like five! We were in the 'friend zone' before there WAS a friend zone!

A ⑦ _____ _____ always had the biggest crush on you. All through high school, the whole ⑧ _____. You were like my fantasy.

B Why ⑨ _____ _____ ever tell me this before? It's ⑩ _____ _____ hear all this from YOU, now.

A I never ⑪ _____ _____ meant anything to you. I thought

I was just your best friend's big brother.

B Well, yeah. You were. THEN. ⑫ _____ _____, you and Michelle are both my best friends. I feel like you're MY …

A Brother?

B Is that so bad?

A Um, yeah … frankly. I mean, I ⑬ _____ think there are very many states where …

B Oh, Carl, ⑭ _____ _____! The timing is not right for this. Not ⑮ _____ _____ _____!

Stage 2 ドラマのシーン解説

日本語訳と、解説を参照しながら、ドラマの内容を確認しよう。そのあとで、Stage1の穴埋めに再チャレンジしてみよう。

A Karen, is there any way I can ① **get out of** the friend zone with you?

カレン、どうにかして、僕と君の関係を友達ゾーンから抜け出させることってできないかな？

* get out of … 「…を抜け出す；出る」　friend zone 「友達関係の領域」

B Oh, Carl! You're so funny!

まあ、カール。あなたっておかしい！

A I guess that … ② **sort of** answers my question, huh?

それって…ある種、僕の質問に対する返答なのかなあ、ねえ？

B ③ **Wait a** minute. You're not serious, are you?

え？ 冗談で言ってるんだよね？

＊ serious「まじめな」

A I am. I mean, I was. I mean, I ④ **wanted** YOU ⑤ **to** think I was being serious.

僕はまじめだよ。というか、真剣だったよ。つまりさ、僕が真剣になってきてるんだって、君に考えてほしかったんだよ。

B Carl! ⑥ **You and I** have known each other since we were like five! We were in the 'friend zone' before there WAS a friend zone!

カール！ あなたと私は5歳くらいからお互いを知ってるのよ！ 友達ゾーンができる前から、私たちは友達ゾーンにいたわけよね！

A ⑦ **But I** always had the biggest crush on you. All through high school, the whole ⑧ **bit**. You were like my fantasy.

でも、僕はいつだって君に夢中だったんだ。高校の間ずっとさ。君にあこがれてたんだ。

＊ crush「夢中」 the whole bit「そのすべて」 fantasy「あこがれの人；空想；夢想」

B Why ⑨ **didn't you** ever tell me this before? It's ⑩ **weird to** hear all this from YOU, now.

どうして、これまで話してくれなかったの？ いまあなたから、そんな告白を受けるのは変よ。

＊ weird「奇妙な」

A I never ⑪ **thought I** meant anything to you. I thought I was just your best friend's big brother.

僕が君にとってのなにかだなんて、思ってもみなかったんだ。僕は、ただの君の親友の兄さんでしかないと思ってた。

B Well, yeah. You were. THEN. ⑫ **But now**, you and Michelle are both my best friends. I feel like you're MY ...

ええ、そうね。そうだったわ。その頃はね。でも、いま、あなたとミシェルはどちらも私の親友なの。私はあなたのことを、自分の…みたいに…

A Brother?

兄弟？

B Is that so bad?

それってそんなにダメかなぁ？

A Um, yeah ... frankly. I mean, I ⑬ **don't** think there are very many states where ...

うーん、うん…正直言うとね。つまりさ、あまり多くの州ではないと思うんだよ、そういう関係を認めてるところって…

* state「（アメリカ合衆国の）州」 I don't think there are very many states where ... このセンテンスは「兄弟同士で恋愛や結婚を認めている州はあまり多くない」という含意。

B Oh, Carl, ⑭ **shut UP**! The timing is not right for this. Not ⑮ **right at ALL**!

ねえ、カール、やめて！ いまはそういうタイミングじゃないわ。まったくね！

Stage 3 英文トランスクリプション

ドラマのシーン全体を英文の原稿で確認しながらCDで耳慣らししよう！ その上で、ドラマ・シーンの音声を聴きながら、まだできていない部分の穴埋めに再チャレンジしよう。

● ● ● ● ● ●

A Karen, is there any way I can ① **get out of** the friend zone with you?

B Oh, Carl! You're so funny!

A I guess that ... ② **sort of** answers my question, huh?

B ③ **Wait a** minute. You're not serious, are you?

A I am. I mean, I was. I mean, I ④ **wanted** YOU ⑤ **to** think I was being serious.

B Carl! ⑥ **You and I** have known each other since we were like five! We were in the 'friend zone' before there WAS a friend zone!

A ⑦ **But I** always had the biggest crush on you. All through high school, the whole ⑧ **bit**. You were like my fantasy.

B Why ⑨ **didn't you** ever tell me this before? It's ⑩ **weird to** hear all this from YOU, now.

A I never ⑪ **thought I** meant anything to you. I thought I was just your best friend's big brother.

B Well, yeah. You were. THEN. ⑫ **But now**, you and Michelle are both my best friends. I feel like you're MY ...

A Brother?

B Is that so bad?

A Um, yeah ... frankly. I mean, I ⑬ **don't** think there are very many states where ...

B Oh, Carl, ⑭ **shut UP**! The timing is not right for this. Not ⑮ **right at ALL**!

Stage 4 音声変化をチェック

まとめとして、穴埋め部分の音声変化の特徴を**スロー・スピード**と**ナチュラル・スピード**で確認しよう。下記に示したカタカナ表記で音声変化を確認して、もう一度ドラマを聴き直してみよう。発音変化のルールは適宜復習しよう。

❶ get out of   ゲット・アウト・ァヴ   ▶ ゲッダ [ラ] ウダ [ラ] (ヴ)
☞ 2カ所の連結部で破裂音 [t] が弾音化する。末尾の [v] 音が脱落することもある。

❷ sort of   ソート・ァヴ   ▶ ソーダ [ラ] ヴ
☞ 連結部で破裂音 [t] が弾音化する。

❸ Wait a   ウェイト・ア   ▶ ウェイダ [ラ]
☞ 連結部で破裂音 [t] が弾音化する。

❹ wanted   ワンティッド   ▶ ワニッ (ド)
☞ 破裂音 [t] が脱落する。末尾の [d] 音が脱落することもある。

❺ to   トゥー   ▶ ドゥ [ル] ー
☞ 破裂音 [t] が弾音化する。

❻ You and I   ユー・アンド・アイ   ▶ ユーアナイ
☞ and の破裂音 [d] が脱落しつつ I に連結する。

❼ But I   バット・アイ   ▶ バッダ [ラ] イ
☞ 連結部で [t] 音が弾音化する。

❽ bit   ビット   ▶ ビッ＿
☞ 末尾の破裂音 [t] が脱落する。

❾ didn't you   ディドゥント・ユー   ▶ ディンチュー
☞ didn't 中程の [d] 音が脱落。連結部の [t] + [j] の部分で音が混じり合い、[チュ] に近い音に変化する。

❿ weird to   ウィアード・トゥー   ▶ ウィアーツ＿トゥー
☞ weird 末尾の破裂音 [d] が脱落する。

⓫ thought I   ソート・アイ   ▶ ソーダ [ラ] イ
☞ 連結部で [t] 音が弾音化する。

⓬ But now   バット・ナウ   ▶ バッ＿ナウ
☞ But 末尾の破裂音 [t] が脱落する。

⓭ don't   ドウント   ▶ ドン＿
☞ don't は弱化。末尾の破裂音 [t] が脱落する。

⓮ shut UP   シャット・アップ   ▶ シャッ＿アップ
☞ shut 末尾の破裂音 [t] が脱落する。

⓯ right at ALL   ライト・アット・オーゥ   ▶ ライダ [ラ] ッド [ロ] ーゥ
☞ 2カ所の連結部で破裂音 [t] が弾音化する。

シングル・コメディー

Unit 4 ホスピタル・ドラマ
Hospital Drama (ER type)

Stage 1 穴埋めドラマ・リスニング

音声変化に注意してCDでドラマの音声を聴きながら空欄部分を埋めてみよう。CDのナチュラル音声での聴き取りが難しいときは、次のトラックに収録されたスロー音声で聴いてみよう。

● ● ● ● ●

A Melissa, you ① _____ _____ come to terms with things. You are not helping when you talk to Greg like he's an eight year old.

B ② _____ tell ME ③ _____ _____ talk to my husband! You just do your job!

A What, exactly, do you think my job is? To change the laws of nature? Your husband has a terminal illness. There is NO cure.

B ④ _____ _____ think I know that? Don't you think that's a bigger issue to us than ⑤ _____ _____ to you?

A Greg is dealing ⑥ _____ _____, Melissa. He accepts it. Right now, he's more worried ⑦ _____ _____, how you are handling this.

B How the hell am I ⑧ _____ _____ 'handle' this, anyway? I suppose you're ⑨ _____ _____ tell me I'm in denial.

A ⑩ _____ _____ think you are. I'm telling you that Greg thinks you are. Every time you go ⑪ _____ _____ he feels

28

like he has to ⑫ _____ _____ a happy face. To protect you.

Ⓑ Well, ⑬ _____ _____ he want? What does he want? This is so unfair!

Ⓐ I know, Melissa. I know it's unfair. It's the unfairest thing in this whole unfair world. But he needs you to face things, ⑭ _____ _____ him.

Ⓑ ⑮ _____ _____ I can't?

Ⓐ You can. You HAVE to.

Stage 2 ドラマのシーン解説

日本語訳と、解説を参照しながら、ドラマの内容を確認しよう。そのあとで、Stage1の穴埋めに再チャレンジしてみよう。

Ⓐ Melissa, you ① **need to** come to terms with things. You are not helping when you talk to Greg like he's an eight year old.

メリッサ、現実を受け入れなきゃだめだよ。グレッグが8歳児かなにかみたいに話をするのはよくないよ。

＊ come to terms with ...「(あきらめて) …を受け入れる」　help「役に立つ」

Ⓑ ② **Don't** tell ME ③ **how to** talk to my husband! You just do your job!

私が夫にどういうふうに話しかけたっていいでしょ！ あなたには関係ないわ！

＊ do one's job「自分の仕事をする」

A What, exactly, do you think my job is? To change the laws of nature? Your husband has a terminal illness. There is NO cure.

君は、いったい僕の仕事がなんだと思ってる？ 自然の法則を変えることだとでも？ 君の夫は病の末期症状なんだよ。治癒の望みはないんだ。

＊ terminal「末期の」 cure「治癒；治療法」

B ④ **Don't you** think I know that? Don't you think that's a bigger issue to us than ⑤ **it is** to you?

私がわかってないとでも思ってるの？ それが、あなたにとってより、私たちにとって大きな問題だとは思わないの？

A Greg is dealing ⑥ **with it**, Melissa. He accepts it. Right now, he's more worried ⑦ **about you**, how you are handling this.

グレッグはそれと闘っているんだよ、メリッサ。彼は受け入れているよ。いま彼は、君のことのほうを心配しているんだよ。君の受け入れ方をね。

＊ deal with ...「…に対処する」 accept「受け入れる」

B How the hell am I ⑧ **supposed to** 'handle' this, anyway? I suppose you're ⑨ **going to** tell me I'm in denial.

じゃあ、私はいったいこれにどうやって対処するべきなのよ？ おそらく、あなたは私が事実を受け入れてないって言うつもりでしょ。

＊ hell は強調。 be supposed to ...「(当然) …することになっている」
　in denial「(心痛を避けるために) 事実を信じずに」

A ⑩ **I don't** think you are. I'm telling you that Greg thinks you are. Every time you go ⑪ **in there** he feels like he has to ⑫ **put on** a happy face. To protect you.

僕は、そうじゃないと思う。だけど、グレッグはそう思ってるんだよ。君が彼の病室に行くたびに、幸福そうな表情をしなきゃって彼は感じているんだ。君をかばうためにね。

* I'm telling you that ... 「よく聞いて；言っておくけど」強調。　protect「守る；かばう；保護する」

Ⓑ Well, ⑬ **what does** he want? What does he want? This is so unfair!

そうね、彼はどうしたいのよ？ なにを望んでるの？ あまりにも不公平よ！

* unfair「不公平な；ずるい」

Ⓐ I know, Melissa. I know it's unfair. It's the unfairest thing in this whole unfair world. But he needs you to face things, ⑭ **right alongside** him.

わかるよ、メリッサ。不公平さ。不公平なこの世の中でももっとも不公平なことだよ。でも、彼は君に現実と向き合ってほしいんだ。彼とぴったり寄り添ってね。

* face「直面する；正視する」　alongside ...「…といっしょに；そばで」

Ⓑ ⑮ **What if** I can't?

できなかったら、どうなるの？

* What if ...?「もし…ならどうなるの？」

Ⓐ You can. You HAVE to.

君ならできるさ。君はそうしなきゃ。

Stage 3　英文トランスクリプション

ドラマのシーン全体を英文の原稿で確認しながらCDで耳慣らししよう！ その上で、ドラマ・シーンの音声を聴きながら、まだできていない部分の穴埋めに再チャレンジしよう。

• • • • •

A Melissa, you ① **need to** come to terms with things. You are not helping when you talk to Greg like he's an eight year old.

B ② **Don't** tell ME ③ **how to** talk to my husband! You just do your job!

A What, exactly, do you think my job is? To change the laws of nature? Your husband has a terminal illness. There is NO cure.

B ④ **Don't you** think I know that? Don't you think that's a bigger issue to us than ⑤ **it is** to you?

A Greg is dealing ⑥ **with it**, Melissa. He accepts it. Right now, he's more worried ⑦ **about you**, how you are handling this.

B How the hell am I ⑧ **supposed to** 'handle' this, anyway? I suppose you're ⑨ **going to** tell me I'm in denial.

A ⑩ **I don't** think you are. I'm telling you that Greg thinks you are. Every time you go ⑪ **in there** he feels like he has to ⑫ **put on** a happy face. To protect you.

B Well, ⑬ **what does** he want? What does he want? This is so unfair!

A I know, Melissa. I know it's unfair. It's the unfairest thing in this whole unfair world. But he needs you to face things, ⑭ **right alongside** him.

B ⑮ **What if** I can't?

A You can. You HAVE to.

32

Stage 4 音声変化をチェック

まとめとして、穴埋め部分の音声変化の特徴を**スロー・スピード**と**ナチュラル・スピード**で確認しよう。下記に示したカタカナ表記で音声変化を確認して、もう一度ドラマを聴き直してみよう。発音変化のルールは適宜復習しよう。

❶ need to　　　　　　　　　　ニード・トゥー　　　　　▶ ニーッ__ドゥ [ル] ─
  ☞ need の破裂音 [d] が脱落する。to の破裂音 [t] が弾音化する。

❷ Don't　　　　　　　　　　　ドウント　　　　　　　　▶ ドン__
  ☞ Don't は弱化。末尾の [t] 音も脱落する。

❸ how to　　　　　　　　　　ハウ・トゥー　　　　　　▶ ハウドゥ [ル] ─
  ☞ to の破裂音 [t] が弾音化する。

❹ Don't you　　　　　　　　ドウント・ユー　　　　　▶ ドンチュー
  ☞ Don't は弱化して [ドント] という発音になる。2語の連結部で [t] + [j] の音が混じり合い、[チュ] に近い音に変化する。

❺ it is　　　　　　　　　　　イット・イズ　　　　　　▶ イッディ [リ] ズ
  ☞ 連結部で [t] 音が弾音化する。

❻ with it　　　　　　　　　　ウィズ・イット　　　　　▶ ウィズィッ__
  ☞ 2語が連結。it 末尾の破裂音 [t] が脱落する。

❼ about you　　　　　　　　アバウト・ユー　　　　　▶ アバウッ__ユー
  ☞ about 末尾の破裂音 [t] が脱落する。

❽ supposed to　　　　　　　サポウズド・トゥー　　　▶ サポウスッ__トゥー
  ☞ supposed の [z] 音が [s] 音に変化する。末尾の [d] 音も脱落。

❾ going to　　　　　　　　　ゴウイング・トゥー　　　▶ ゴウイン__トゥー
  ☞ going の破裂音 [g] が脱落する。

❿ I don't　　　　　　　　　　アイ・ドウント　　　　　▶ アイドン__
  ☞ don't は弱化。末尾の [t] 音も脱落する。

⓫ in there　　　　　　　　　イン・ゼア　　　　　　　▶ イネァ
  ☞ [n] + [ð] が [n] 音に変化する。

⓬ put on　　　　　　　　　　プット・オン　　　　　　▶ プッド [ロ] ン
  ☞ 連結部で [t] 音が弾音化する。

⓭ what does　　　　　　　　ワット・ダズ　　　　　　▶ ワッ__ダズ
  ☞ what 末尾の破裂音 [t] が脱落する。

⓮ right alongside　　　　　ライト・アロングサイド　▶ ライダ [ラ] ロングサイド
  ☞ 2語が連結。連結部で [t] 音が弾音化する。

⓯ What if　　　　　　　　　ワット・イフ　　　　　　▶ ワッディ [リ] フ
  ☞ 2語が連結。連結部で [t] 音が弾音化する。

Unit 5 政治ドラマ
Political Drama (West Wing type)

Stage 1 穴埋めドラマ・リスニング

音声変化に注意してCDでドラマの音声を聴きながら空欄部分を埋めてみよう。CDのナチュラル音声での聴き取りが難しいときは、次のトラックに収録されたスロー音声で聴いてみよう。

● ● ● ● ●

A ① _____ _____ will give the most ② _____ speech of your ③ _____ career. Possibly one of the most important speeches in the history of our republic.

B You mean this is my 'Gettysburg moment,' huh?

A ④ _____ _____ be that. You have to ⑤ _____ _____.

B Gail, ⑥ _____ _____ _____ _____ this country? Why does it seem that every generation faces a crisis that threatens to ⑦ _____ _____ in two?

A Just democracy, messy old democracy. Fifty cantankerous states, and two political ⑧ _____ that ⑨ _____ _____ ⑩ _____ each other.

B Well, ONE political ⑪ _____ wants to destroy ME, that's for sure. And they've just about succeeded. One ⑫ _____ speech won't change that.

A Mr. President, I'm ⑬ _____ _____ _____. I have served

under four administrations. And I've never had more confidence in a leader ⑭ _____ _____ have in you right now.

B Gail, this morning, about five o'clock, just after I finished the final draft, I took a walk through the picture gallery. I looked into the eyes of all those faces of all those men who've been in these shoes before me.

A And ... did they tell you anything?

B Not really. They just reminded me that one day, that's all I'll be too. Just a ⑮ _____ on that wall.

Stage 2 ドラマのシーン解説

日本語訳と、解説を参照しながら、ドラマの内容を確認しよう。そのあとで、Stage1の穴埋めに再チャレンジしてみよう。

A ① **Tonight you** will give the most ② **important** speech of your ③ **political** career. Possibly one of the most important speeches in the history of our republic.

今夜あなたは、ご自身の政界でのキャリアでもっとも重要なスピーチをなさいます。わが共和国の歴史でも、もっとも重要なスピーチのひとつかもしれません。

B You mean this is my 'Gettysburg moment,' huh?

つまり君は、これをゲッティスバーグの演説に匹敵する瞬間だと?

* Gettysburg = Gettysburg Address「ゲッティスバーグの演説」リンカーン大統領が行った「人民の、人民による、人民のための政治」というフレーズで有名な演説。

政治ドラマ　35

A ④ **It can** be that. You have to ⑤ **own it**.

そうなるかもしれません。ご自身でそれをつかみ取らなければなりません。

* own「所有する；手にする」

B Gail, ⑥ **what is it about** this country? Why does it seem that every generation faces a crisis that threatens to ⑦ **split us** in two?

ゲイル、この国はどうなのだろう？ どうして、すべての世代が国論を二分させるような危機に直面するように思えるのだろう？

* what is it about ...?「…はどうだろう?」感想を聞く表現。　generation「世代」　crisis「危機」　threaten to ...「…する恐れがある」　split ... in two「二分する；ふたつに裂く」

A Just democracy, messy old democracy. Fifty cantankerous states, and two political ⑧ **parties** that ⑨ **want to** ⑩ **destroy** each other.

民主主義です。不快で古くさい民主主義ゆえですよ。50 の不平でいっぱいの州と、互いを潰したがっているふたつの政党が問題なのです。

* messy「不快な」　cantankerous「文句の多い；怒りっぽい」

B Well, ONE political ⑪ **party** wants to destroy ME, that's for sure. And they've just about succeeded. One ⑫ **little** speech won't change that.

そうだね、ひとつの政党が私を潰したがっているのは確かだ。そして、彼らはほぼ成功している。たった一度の小さなスピーチでは変えようがないさ。

* just about「ほとんど；だいたい」

A Mr. President, I'm ⑬ **an old timer**. I have served under four administrations. And I've never had more confidence in a leader ⑭ **than I** have in you right now.

大統領閣下、私は古株で、4つの政権に仕えてきました。そして、まさにいま、どの指導者にもおかなかったほどの信頼を、あなたにおいているのです。

* old timer「老人；古参」

B Gail, this morning, about five o'clock, just after I finished the final draft, I took a walk through the picture gallery. I looked into the eyes of all those faces of all those men who've been in these shoes before me.

ゲイル、今朝5時頃、ちょうど、最終原稿を仕上げたすぐあとに、画廊を散歩したんだよ。私の前に、大統領の職を務めたすべての男の顔の目を覗き込んだんだ。

* final draft「最終原稿」 men who've been in these shoes「この靴を履いた男たち」ここでは、自分と同じ役職、つまり大統領を務めた人を指す。

A And ... did they tell you anything?

で…彼らはなにか言いましたか？

B Not really. They just reminded me that one day, that's all I'll be too. Just a ⑮ **picture** on that wall.

いや。ただ彼らは思い出させてくれただけさ。いつの日か私もそれになるだけだとね。あの壁のただの一枚の絵にさ。

* remind someone that ...「…に…ということを思い出させる」 that's all ...「それが…のすべてだ」

政治ドラマ　37

Stage 3 英文トランスクリプション

ドラマのシーン全体を英文の原稿で確認しながらCDで耳慣らししよう！ その上で、ドラマ・シーンの音声を聴きながら、まだできていない部分の穴埋めに再チャレンジしよう。

• • • • • •

Ⓐ ① **Tonight you** will give the most ② **important** speech of your ③ **political** career. Possibly one of the most important speeches in the history of our republic.

Ⓑ You mean this is my 'Gettysburg moment,' huh?

Ⓐ ④ **It can** be that. You have to ⑤ **own it**.

Ⓑ Gail, ⑥ **what is it about** this country? Why does it seem that every generation faces a crisis that threatens to ⑦ **split us** in two?

Ⓐ Just democracy, messy old democracy. Fifty cantankerous states, and two political ⑧ **parties** that ⑨ **want to** ⑩ **destroy** each other.

Ⓑ Well, ONE political ⑪ **party** wants to destroy ME, that's for sure. And they've just about succeeded. One ⑫ **little** speech won't change that.

Ⓐ Mr. President, I'm ⑬ **an old timer**. I have served under four administrations. And I've never had more confidence in a leader ⑭ **than I** have in you right now.

Ⓑ Gail, this morning, about five o'clock, just after I finished the final draft, I took a walk through the picture gallery. I looked into the eyes of all those faces of all those men who've been in these shoes before me.

Ⓐ And ... did they tell you anything?

Ⓑ Not really. They just reminded me that one day, that's all I'll be too. Just a ⑮ **picture** on that wall.

Stage 4 音声変化をチェック

まとめとして、穴埋め部分の音声変化の特徴を**スロー・スピード**と**ナチュラル・スピード**で確認しよう。下記に示したカタカナ表記で音声変化を確認して、もう一度ドラマを聴き直してみよう。発音変化のルールは適宜復習しよう。

❶ **Tonight you**　　　　　　　トゥナイト・ユー　　　　▶ トゥナイチュー
　☞ [t]＋[j] の部分で音が混じり合い、[チュ] に近い音に変化する。

❷ **important**　　　　　　　　イムポートゥント　　　　▶ イムポーんン＿
　☞ [tn] の [t] 音が声門閉鎖音化する。末尾の破裂音 [t] も脱落。

❸ **political**　　　　　　　　ポリティカゥ　　　　　　▶ ポリディ [リ] カゥ
　☞ 破裂音 [t] 音が弾音化する。

❹ **It can**　　　　　　　　　　イット・キャン　　　　　▶ イッ＿キャン
　☞ it 末尾の破裂音 [t] が脱落する。

❺ **own it**　　　　　　　　　　オウン・イット　　　　　▶ オウニッ＿
　☞ 2 語が連結。it 末尾の破裂音 [t] が脱落する。

❻ **what is it about**　　　　ワット・イズ・イット・アバウト
　　　　　　　　　　　　　　　　　　　　　　　　　　　　▶ ワッディ [リ] ズィッダ [ラ] バウッ＿
　☞ 4 語が連結。what is と it about の連結部で [t] 音が弾音化する。about 末尾の破裂音 [t] が脱落する。

❼ **split us**　　　　　　　　スプリット・アス　　　　▶ スプリッダ [ラ] ス
　☞ 連結部で [t] 音が弾音化する。

❽ **parties**　　　　　　　　　パーティーズ　　　　　　▶ パーディ [リ] ーズ
　☞ 破裂音 [t] が弾音化する。

❾ **want to**　　　　　　　　　ワント・トゥー　　　　　▶ ワン＿トゥー
　☞ want 末尾の破裂音 [t] が脱落する。

❿ **destroy**　　　　　　　　　デストゥロイ　　　　　　▶ デスチュロイ
　☞ [tr] 部分の [t] 音が [チュ] に近い音に変化する。

⓫ **party**　　　　　　　　　　パーティー　　　　　　　▶ パーディ [リ] ー
　☞ 破裂音 [t] が弾音化する。

⓬ **little**　　　　　　　　　 リトゥゥ　　　　　　　　▶ リドゥ [ル] ゥ
　☞ 破裂音 [t] が弾音化する。

⓭ **an old timer**　　　　　　アン・オウゥド・タイマー　▶ アノウゥ＿タイマー
　☞ an old は連結。old 末尾の破裂音 [d] が脱落する。

⓮ **than I**　　　　　　　　　 ザン・アイ　　　　　　　▶ ザナイ
　☞ 2 語が連結する。

⓯ **picture**　　　　　　　　　ピクチャー　　　　　　　▶ ピクシャー
　☞ 破裂音 [t] が脱落する。

政治ドラマ　39

Unit 6　SF ドラマ

Sci-Fi Drama (Star Trek type)

Stage 1　穴埋めドラマ・リスニング

音声変化に注意してCDでドラマの音声を聴きながら空欄部分を埋めてみよう。CDのナチュラル音声での聴き取りが難しいときは、次のトラックに収録されたスロー音声で聴いてみよう。

● ● ● ● ●

A Captain, I am ① _____ _____ get some initial readings ② _____ _____ vessel that's been ③ _____ us.

B Good work, Lieutenant. ④ _____ _____ _____ got so far?

A Not much, sir. Whoever's inside is doing a good job of ⑤ _____ _____. One thing seems clear, though. The technology seems very advanced.

B More than our own?

A I can't say for sure, ⑥ _____ _____ _____ _____ a good bet.

B Any clues if they have weapons ⑦ _____ _____ _____ ?

A No clues whatsoever, sir. Nor any idea ⑧ _____ _____ _____ weaponry they may be using.

B Okay, I'm ⑨ _____ _____ initiate contact. ⑩ _____ _____ ⑪ _____ _____ frequencies.

A Yes, sir. Ready when you are.

40

B This is the captain of the vessel you have been following. We have no hostile intentions. Furthermore, we are ⑫ _____ _____ of any claims upon this sector of the galaxy. If you feel ⑬ _____ ⑭ _____ _____ entered into your territory unknowingly, please send a peaceful reply to any frequency you receive this message on.

A Sent, sir. So, now we just wait?

B Yes, and keep all channels open.

A Roger, sir. Oh, wait. Something is coming in now! It's … it's quite belligerent, sir. They are demanding ⑮ _____ _____ and unconditional surrender!

Stage 2 ドラマのシーン解説

日本語訳と、解説を参照しながら、ドラマの内容を確認しよう。そのあとで、Stage1の穴埋めに再チャレンジしてみよう。

A Captain, I am ① **starting to** get some initial readings ② **on the** vessel that's been ③ **shadowing** us.

キャプテン、われわれを追尾している船の初期計測を開始するところです。

＊ reading「計器などで計測すること」 vessel「船；宇宙船」 shadow「尾行する」

B Good work, Lieutenant. ④ **What have you** got so far?

よろしい、中尉。これまでにわかったことは？

＊ so far「これまでに」

A Not much, sir. Whoever's inside is doing a good job of

⑤ **cloaking her**. One thing seems clear, though. The technology seems very advanced.

まだあまり。中にいるのがだれであれ、船の隠蔽に関していい仕事をしていますね。ただ、ひとつだけはっきりしているようなのですが。技術がとても進んでいるようなのです。

* cloak「覆い隠す；隠蔽する」 advanced「進歩した；上級の」

Ⓑ More than our own?

われわれ以上にかい？

Ⓐ I can't say for sure, ⑥ **but that would be** a good bet.

はっきりは申し上げられませんが、そう判断するのが妥当でしょう。

* that would be a good bet「そう考えて間違いないだろう」

Ⓑ Any clues if they have weapons ⑦ **trained on us**?

われわれに武器の照準を定めているかどうか知る手がかりはなにかあるのか？

* clue「手がかり；糸口」 train on ...「（武器などを）…に向ける」

Ⓐ No clues whatsoever, sir. Nor any idea ⑧ **what sort of** weaponry they may be using.

まったくありません。彼らがどのような兵器を使っているのかもさっぱりわかりません。

* no ... whatsoever「少しの…もない」 Nor ...「…もない」 sort「種類」 weaponry「兵器類」

Ⓑ Okay, I'm ⑨ **going to** initiate contact. ⑩ **Put this** ⑪ **on all** frequencies.

わかった。私が接触を開始してみよう。これを全周波数に乗せてくれ。

* initiate「始める；着手する」 frequency「周波数」

Ⓐ Yes, sir. Ready when you are.

了解しました。いつでもどうぞ。

* Ready when you are. 「(あなたが準備できたら) いつでもどうぞ」

Ⓑ This is the captain of the vessel you have been following. We have no hostile intentions. Furthermore, we are ⑫ **not aware** of any claims upon this sector of the galaxy. If you feel ⑬ **that** ⑭ **we have** entered into your territory unknowingly, please send a peaceful reply to any frequency you receive this message on.

こちら、貴艦が追尾している船のキャプテンです。われわれには敵意はありません。さらに、われわれは宇宙のこのエリアの領有権を認識していません。われわれが図らずもあなた方の領域に入ったと感じているのなら、このメッセージを受信した周波数に平和的な応答を送ってください。

* hostile intentions「敵意」 claim「土地・財産などの権利；領有権」 sector「地域」
  territory「領地」 unknowingly「知らないで；意図せず」

Ⓐ Sent, sir. So, now we just wait?

送信しました、キャプテン。で、われわれは待っているだけですね？

Ⓑ Yes, and keep all channels open.

ああ、すべてのチャンネルをオープンに保ってくれ。

* channel「通信チャンネル；周波数帯」

Ⓐ Roger, sir. Oh, wait. Something is coming in now! It's ... it's quite belligerent, sir. They are demanding ⑮ **an immediate** and unconditional surrender!

了解。あ、待ってください。いまなにか入ってきています！ こ…これは、とても好戦的なメッセージです。彼らは、即刻の無条件降伏を要求しています！

* belligerent「好戦的な；敵意に満ちた」 unconditional surrender「無条件降伏」

Stage 3 英文トランスクリプション

ドラマのシーン全体を英文の原稿で確認しながらCDで耳慣らししよう！ その上で、ドラマ・シーンの音声を聴きながら、まだできていない部分の穴埋めに再チャレンジしよう。

● ● ● ● ● ●

A Captain, I am ① **starting to** get some initial readings ② **on the** vessel that's been ③ **shadowing** us.

B Good work, Lieutenant. ④ **What have you** got so far?

A Not much, sir. Whoever's inside is doing a good job of ⑤ **cloaking her**. One thing seems clear, though. The technology seems very advanced.

B More than our own?

A I can't say for sure, ⑥ **but that would be** a good bet.

B Any clues if they have weapons ⑦ **trained on us**?

A No clues whatsoever, sir. Nor any idea ⑧ **what sort of** weaponry they may be using.

B Okay, I'm ⑨ **going to** initiate contact. ⑩ **Put this** ⑪ **on all** frequencies.

A Yes, sir. Ready when you are.

B This is the captain of the vessel you have been following. We have no hostile intentions. Furthermore, we are ⑫ **not aware** of any claims upon this sector of the galaxy. If you feel ⑬ **that** ⑭ **we have** entered into your territory unknowingly, please send a peaceful reply to any frequency you receive this message on.

A Sent, sir. So, now we just wait?

B Yes, and keep all channels open.

A Roger, sir. Oh, wait. Something is coming in now! It's ... it's quite belligerent, sir. They are demanding ⑮ **an immediate** and unconditional surrender!

Stage 4 音声変化をチェック

まとめとして、穴埋め部分の音声変化の特徴を**スロー・スピード**と**ナチュラル・スピード**で確認しよう。下記に示したカタカナ表記で音声変化を確認して、もう一度ドラマを聴き直してみよう。発音変化のルールは適宜復習しよう。

❶ starting to スターティング・トゥー ▶ スターティン_トゥー
☞ starting 末尾の破裂音 [g] が脱落する。

❷ on the オン・ザ ▶ オナ
☞ [n] + [ð] が [n] 音に変化する。

❸ shadowing シャドウイング ▶ シャド [ロ] ウイング
☞ 破裂音 [d] 音が弾音化することがある。

❹ What have you ワット・ハヴ・ユー ▶ ワッダ [ラ] ヴユー
☞ what have の連結部で破裂音 [t] が弾音化する。

❺ cloaking her クローキング・ハー ▶ クローキンガー
☞ cloaking が、弱化した her [アー] に連結する。

❻ but that would be バット・ザット・ウッド・ビー ▶ バッ_ザッ_ウッ_ビー
☞ but that would 3 語の末尾の破裂音が、それぞれ脱落する。

❼ trained on us トゥレインド・オン・アス ▶ トゥレインドナス
☞ 3 語が連結。trained の [tr] 部分の [t] 音が [チュ] に近い音に変化することもある。

❽ what sort of ワット・ソート・アヴ ▶ ワッ_ソーダ [ラ] ヴ
☞ what 末尾の破裂音 [t] が脱落する。sort of の連結部で破裂音 [t] が弾音化する。

❾ going to ゴウイング・トゥー ▶ ゴウイヌー
☞ going 末尾の破裂音 [g] が脱落しつつ、弱化した to [トゥー] に連結する。

❿ Put this プット・ズィス ▶ プッ_ズィス
☞ put 末尾の破裂音 [t] が脱落する。

⓫ on all オン・オーゥ ▶ オノーゥ
☞ 2 語が連結する。

⓬ not aware ナット・アウェアー ▶ ナッダ [ラ] ウェアー
☞ 2 語が連結する。連結部で破裂音 [t] が弾音化する。

⓭ that ザット ▶ _アッ_
☞ that が弱化し頭の [ð] 音と、末尾の [t] が脱落する。

⓮ we have ウィ・ハヴ ▶ ウィ_アヴ
☞ have が弱化して [h] 音が脱落する。

⓯ an immediate アン・イミーディアト ▶ アニミーディア (ト)
☞ 2 語が連結する。末尾の [t] 音が脱落することもある。

SF ドラマ

Unit 7 法律コメディー
Legal Comedy (Ally McBeal type)

Stage 1 穴埋めドラマ・リスニング

音声変化に注意してCDでドラマの音声を聴きながら空欄部分を埋めてみよう。CDのナチュラル音声での聴き取りが難しいときは、次のトラックに収録されたスロー音声で聴いてみよう。

● ● ● ● ●

A ① _____ makes you so sure Mrs. Stafford is ② _____ _____ truth?

B What makes YOU think she isn't?

A There've been rumors of Don Stafford's ③ _____ for years now. He has a reputation as a womanizer.

B So she ④ _____ _____ file for divorce until his stock was ⑤ _____ _____ highest. She ⑥ _____ _____ cards right. Maybe ⑦ _____ _____ ethical, ⑧ _____ so what?

A Jake, ⑨ _____ _____ think the timing of that video his ⑩ _____ released of the two of them in a ⑪ _____ _____ was just a tad convenient? Just when the Staffords have been talking about selling their ⑫ _____ franchise?

B ⑬ _____ _____ minute, …? You think Fran Stafford is in cahoots with the mistress … what's her name … Valencia?

A Valeria. Look, Valeria is a failed 'actress.' Her career was basically kaput. All she gets from releasing that video is fifteen more minutes of fame, but LOTS of public shaming. Unless ...

B Unless she and Fran Stafford have a private arrangement? I see where you're going.

A Why not? Her husband has been publicly humiliated. Mrs. Stafford can renegotiate the sales of the football team on HER terms. She ⑭ _____ _____ an extra ⑮ _____ million. That's enough to keep Valeria in bikini wax and hair extensions forever.

Stage 2 ドラマのシーン解説

日本語訳と、解説を参照しながら、ドラマの内容を確認しよう。そのあとで、Stage1の穴埋めに再チャレンジしてみよう。

A ① **What** makes you so sure Mrs. Stafford is ② **telling the** truth?

どうして、スタフォード夫人がホントのことを言ってるってそんなに確信してるの？

＊ sure「確信して」

B What makes YOU think she isn't?

どうして、君はそうじゃないって思ってるんだい？

A There've been rumors of Don Stafford's ③ **infidelity** for years now. He has a reputation as a womanizer.

ドン・スタフォードにはもう何年も不貞のうわさがあるのよ。女たらしだって評判なの。

法律コメディー 47

＊ infidelity「不貞」 womanizer「女たらし；プレイボーイ」

Ⓑ So she ④ **waited to** file for divorce until his stock was ⑤ **at its** highest. She ⑥ **played her** cards right. Maybe ⑦ **not exactly** ethical, ⑧ **but** so what?

だから、彼女はドンの株が最高値になるまで待って離婚訴訟をしたんだよ。的確なカードを切ったってことさ。たぶん道徳的とは言えないけど、それがなんだってのさ？

＊ ethical「道義にかなった」

Ⓐ Jake, ⑨ **don't you** think the timing of that video his ⑩ **mistress** released of the two of them in a ⑪ **hot tub** was just a tad convenient? Just when the Staffords have been talking about selling their ⑫ **football** franchise?

ジェイク、彼の愛人が、ふたりがお風呂に入っているあのビデオを公開したタイミングが、ちょっと都合がいいって思わないの？ちょうど夫妻がアメフトのチームを売りに出す話をしていたときなんでしょ？

＊ mistress「愛人」 hot tub「温水浴槽」 football franchise「プロのアメフト・チーム」

Ⓑ ⑬ **Wait a** minute, …? You think Fran Stafford is in cahoots with the mistress … what's her name … Valencia?

ちょっと待ってよ……？ 君はフラン・スタフォードがその愛人、なんて名前だっけ…バレンシア？ と共謀してるって思ってるんだね？

＊ in cahoots「共謀して」

Ⓐ Valeria. Look, Valeria is a failed 'actress.' Her career was basically kaput. All she gets from releasing that video is fifteen more minutes of fame, but LOTS of public shaming. Unless …

バレリアよ。あのね、バレリアは売れない女優なの。女優としてのキャリアは、基本的にも

うおしまいだったのよ。あのビデオを公開して彼女が得られるすべてのものと言えば、追加の 15 分だけの名声よ、でも公にものすごい恥をさらすのよ。でも、もし…

* failed「失敗した；成功しなかった」 kaput「もはや立ち直れない」 shaming「不名誉；恥さらし」
 unless ...「…でない限りは」

B Unless she and Fran Stafford have a private arrangement? I see where you're going.

彼女とフラン・スタフォードが個人的な取り決めをしていない限りは？ 君の話が見えてきたよ。

A Why not? Her husband has been publicly humiliated. Mrs. Stafford can renegotiate the sales of the football team on HER terms. She ⑭ **might make** an extra ⑮ **forty** million. That's enough to keep Valeria in bikini wax and hair extensions forever.

当然よ。彼女の夫は公に辱めを受けているのよ。スタフォード夫人は彼女の好きな条件でアメフト・チームの売買を再交渉できるわ。彼女は余分に 4 千万ドル稼げるかもしれないの。それだけあれば、永遠にバレリアのビキニ・ラインをワックス脱毛させて、エクステをつけさせるのに十分なのよ。

* Why not?「当然だ；そうでないわけがない」 humiliate「恥をかかせる」
 on someone's terms「…の好きな条件で」

Stage 3 英文トランスクリプション

ドラマのシーン全体を英文の原稿で確認しながらCDで耳慣らししよう！ その上で、ドラマ・シーンの音声を聴きながら、まだできていない部分の穴埋めに再チャレンジしよう。

● ● ● ● ● ●

A ① **What** makes you so sure Mrs. Stafford is ② **telling the** truth?

B What makes YOU think she isn't?

A There've been rumors of Don Stafford's ③ **infidelity** for years now. He has a reputation as a womanizer.

B So she ④ **waited to** file for divorce until his stock was ⑤ **at its** highest. She ⑥ **played her** cards right. Maybe ⑦ **not exactly** ethical, ⑧ **but** so what?

A Jake, ⑨ **don't you** think the timing of that video his ⑩ **mistress** released of the two of them in a ⑪ **hot tub** was just a tad convenient? Just when the Staffords have been talking about selling their ⑫ **football** franchise?

B ⑬ **Wait a** minute, …? You think Fran Stafford is in cahoots with the mistress … what's her name … Valencia?

A Valeria. Look, Valeria is a failed 'actress.' Her career was basically kaput. All she gets from releasing that video is fifteen more minutes of fame, but LOTS of public shaming. Unless …

B Unless she and Fran Stafford have a private arrangement? I see where you're going.

A Why not? Her husband has been publicly humiliated. Mrs. Stafford can renegotiate the sales of the football team on HER terms. She ⑭ **might make** an extra ⑮ **forty** million. That's enough to keep Valeria in bikini wax and hair extensions forever.

Stage 4 　音声変化をチェック

まとめとして、穴埋め部分の音声変化の特徴を**スロー・スピード**と**ナチュラル・スピード**で確認しよう。下記に示したカタカナ表記で音声変化を確認して、もう一度ドラマを聴き直してみよう。発音変化のルールは適宜復習しよう。

❶ What　　　　　　　　　ワット　　　　　　　▶ ワッ＿
☞ 末尾の [t] 音が脱落する。

❷ telling the　　　　　　テリング・ザ　　　　▶ テリナ
☞ telling 末尾の [g] が脱落。[n] + [ð] が [n] 音に変化する。

❸ infidelity　　　　　　インフィデリティー　　▶ インフィデリディ [リ] ー
☞ 破裂音 [t] が弾音化する。

❹ waited to　　　　　　ウェイティッド・トゥー　▶ ウェイディ [リ] ッ＿トゥー
☞ waited の破裂音 [t] が弾音化する。末尾の [d] 音も脱落。

❺ at its　　　　　　　　アット・イッツ　　　　▶ アッディ [リ] ッツ
☞ 連結部の破裂音 [t] が弾音化する。

❻ played her　　　　　プレイド・ハー　　　　▶ プレイダー
☞ played が弱化した her [アー] に連結する。

❼ not exactly　　　　　ナット・エクザクトゥーリー　▶ ナッデ[レ] クザク(トゥ) リー
☞ 連結部で [t] 音が弾音化する。exactly の [t] 音が脱落することもある。

❽ but　　　　　　　　　　バット　　　　　　　▶ バッ＿
☞ 末尾の [t] 音が脱落する。

❾ don't you　　　　　　ドウント・ユー　　　　▶ ドンチュー
☞ [t] + [j] の部分で音が混じり合い、[チュ] に近い音に変化する。

❿ mistress　　　　　　ミストゥレス　　　　　▶ ミスチュレス
☞ [tr] 部分の [t] 音が [チュ] に近い音に変化する。

⓫ hot tub　　　　　　　ハット・タブ　　　　　▶ ハッ＿タブ
☞ 破裂音の連続で [t] 音が片方脱落する。

⓬ football　　　　　　フットボーゥ　　　　　▶ フッ＿ボーゥ
☞ 破裂音の [t] [b] の連続で、[t] 音が脱落する。

⓭ Wait a　　　　　　　ウェイト・ア　　　　　▶ ウェイダ [ラ]
☞ 連結部で [t] 音が弾音化する。

⓮ might make　　　　マイト・メイク　　　　▶ マイッ＿メイク
☞ might の破裂音 [t] が脱落する。

⓯ forty　　　　　　　　フォーティー　　　　　▶ フォーディ [リ] ー
☞ 破裂音 [t] が弾音化する。

法律コメディー　51

Unit 8 対テロリスト・ドラマ
Hostage/Terrorist Drama (24 type)

Stage 1 穴埋めドラマ・リスニング

音声変化に注意してCDでドラマの音声を聴きながら空欄部分を埋めてみよう。CDのナチュラル音声での聴き取りが難しいときは、次のトラックに収録されたスロー音声で聴いてみよう。

● ● ● ● ●

A This is Captain Frank Severin of the LAPD hostage negotiation unit. Who am I ① _____ _____ ?

B You ② _____ _____ my name, Frankie. You just call me TNT. You ③ _____ _____ ?

A Yeah, I got that.

B You got that what?

A I ④ _____ _____, TNT.

B That's ⑤ _____, Frankie, 'cuz I have enough TNT ⑥ _____ blow this building up.

A Look, nobody has to get hurt ... you just tell me how you want this to go.

B Okay, first, there's a helicopter ⑦ _____ _____ this building. That breaks my concentration, Frankie. I ⑧ _____ _____ gone, poof! The buzzing makes me crazy, like I ⑨ _____ _____ pop some of these innocent people here.

A I got you, TNT. (To his team) Move the chopper back to a mile

52

radius!

B Next, I ⑩ _____ _____ to fill up a suitcase with ten million dollars ⑪ _____ _____.

A TNT, we ⑫ _____ _____ take this a ⑬ _____ slower. First, ⑭ _____ _____ know how many hostages you have with you.

B I ask the questions, Frankie. Understand? You ask me one more question, and this lady in ⑮ _____ _____ me who's pissing her pants right now is gonna meet her Maker. You got that?

A Okay, TNT. It's your show.

Stage 2 ドラマのシーン解説

日本語訳と、解説を参照しながら、ドラマの内容を確認しよう。そのあとで、Stage1の穴埋めに再チャレンジしてみよう。

A This is Captain Frank Severin of the LAPD hostage negotiation unit. Who am I ① **speaking to**?

こちらはロス市警の人質交渉班、フランク・セヴリン警部だ。私が話しかけているのはだれだ？

＊ hostage「人質」　negotiation「交渉」

B You ② **don't need** my name, Frankie. You just call me TNT. You ③ **got that**?

俺の名前は必要ないよ、フランキー。TNTとだけ呼べばいい。わかったか？

＊ get「理解する；了解する」

A Yeah, I got that.

ああ、わかったよ。

B You got that what?

わかったって？ それから？

A I ④ **got that**, TNT.

了解だ、TNT。

B That's ⑤ **better**, Frankie, 'cuz I have enough TNT ⑥ **to** blow this building up.

よくなったな、フランキー、なぜかって俺はこのビルを吹っ飛ばすのに十分なTNTを持っているんだからな。

* 'cuz ... = because ...「なぜなら…だから」　TNT「火薬」　blow up「爆破する；吹っ飛ばす」

A Look, nobody has to get hurt ... you just tell me how you want this to go.

聞いてくれ、負傷者は出してはダメだ…お前は、私にどうしたいのかを言ってくれるだけでいい。

* get hurt「負傷する」　how you want this to go「お前がこれをどのように進展させたいか」

B Okay, first, there's a helicopter ⑦ **buzzing around** this building. That breaks my concentration, Frankie. I ⑧ **want it** gone, poof! The buzzing makes me crazy, like I ⑨ **want to** pop some of these innocent people here.

いいだろう、まずはこのビルの周辺をブンブン飛び回っているヘリがいるな。あれが俺の集中を壊してるんだよ、フランキー。あれをどっかにやってくれよ、ピューッと！ ブンブンって音が頭にくるんだよ、この罪のないここにいる奴ら何人かを撃ち殺したい感じになるのさ。

* buzz around「ブンブン飛び回る」　concentration「集中力；集中」　poof「ピュー；フーッ」
　pop「撃ち殺す」　innocent「罪のない；関わりのない」

A I got you, TNT. (To his team) Move the chopper back to a mile radius!

わかった、TNT。（チームに向かって）半径1マイルまでヘリを後退させるんだ！

* chopper「ヘリコプター」　radius「半径」

B Next, I ⑩ **want you** to fill up a suitcase with ten million dollars ⑪ **in it**.

次に、スーツケースに1千万ドルを詰め込め。

* fill up「いっぱいにする」

A TNT, we ⑫ **got to** take this a ⑬ **little** slower. First, ⑭ **let me** know how many hostages you have with you.

TNT、もう少し落ち着いて話をしよう。まず、人質が何人いるのか教えてくれないか。

* let someone know「…に知らせる；教える」

B I ask the questions, Frankie. Understand? You ask me one more question, and this lady in ⑮ **front of** me who's pissing her pants right now is gonna meet her Maker. You got that?

質問はこちらがするんだよ、フランキー。わかったか？　もう一度、俺に質問したら、ちょうどいまこの俺の目の前でズボンに小便を漏らしているレディーは、神さまとご対面することになる。わかったか？

* piss「小便で濡らす；小便をする」　meet one's Maker「死ぬ」Maker は「神」のこと。

A Okay, TNT. It's your show.

了解だ、TNT。お前の言うとおりにする。

対テロリスト・ドラマ　55

Stage 3 英文トランスクリプション

ドラマのシーン全体を英文の原稿で確認しながらCDで耳慣らしししよう！ その上で、ドラマ・シーンの音声を聴きながら、まだできていない部分の穴埋めに再チャレンジしよう。

● ● ● ● ● ●

A This is Captain Frank Severin of the LAPD hostage negotiation unit. Who am I ① **speaking to**?

B You ② **don't need** my name, Frankie. You just call me TNT. You ③ **got that**?

A Yeah, I got that.

B You got that what?

A I ④ **got that**, TNT.

B That's ⑤ **better**, Frankie, 'cuz I have enough TNT ⑥ **to** blow this building up.

A Look, nobody has to get hurt … you just tell me how you want this to go.

B Okay, first, there's a helicopter ⑦ **buzzing around** this building. That breaks my concentration, Frankie. I ⑧ **want it** gone, poof! The buzzing makes me crazy, like I ⑨ **want to** pop some of these innocent people here.

A I got you, TNT. (To his team) Move the chopper back to a mile radius!

B Next, I ⑩ **want you** to fill up a suitcase with ten million dollars ⑪ **in it**.

A TNT, we ⑫ **got to** take this a ⑬ **little** slower. First, ⑭ **let me** know how many hostages you have with you.

B I ask the questions, Frankie. Understand? You ask me one more question, and this lady in ⑮ **front of** me who's pissing her pants right now is gonna meet her Maker. You got that?

A Okay, TNT. It's your show.

Stage 4 音声変化をチェック

まとめとして、穴埋め部分の音声変化の特徴を**スロー・スピード**と**ナチュラル・スピード**で確認しよう。下記に示したカタカナ表記で音声変化を確認して、もう一度ドラマを聴き直してみよう。発音変化のルールは適宜復習しよう。

❶ **speaking to**　　　スピーキング・トゥー　　▶ スピーキン_トゥー
　☞ speaking の破裂音 [g] が脱落する。

❷ **don't need**　　　ドウント・ニード　　▶ ドン_ニード
　☞ don't の破裂音 [t] が脱落する。

❸ **got that**　　　ガット・ザット　　▶ ガッ_ザッ(ト)
　☞ got や that 末尾の破裂音 [t] が脱落する。

❹ **got that**　　　ガット・ザット　　▶ ガッ_ザッ(ト)
　☞ ❸ と同様の変化が起こる。

❺ **better**　　　ベター　　▶ ベダ[ラ]ー
　☞ 破裂音 [t] が弾音化する。

❻ **to**　　　トゥー　　▶ ドゥ[ル]
　☞ 弱化しつつ、破裂音 [t] が弾音化する。

❼ **buzzing around**　　　バズィング・アラウンド　　▶ バズィナラウン_
　☞ buzzing の [g] 音が脱落しつつ 2 語が連結。around 末尾の [d] 音も脱落する。

❽ **want it**　　　ワント・イット　　▶ ワニッ_
　☞ 2 語が連結。want と it の両方で破裂音 [t] が脱落する。

❾ **want to**　　　ワント・トゥー　　▶ ワナ
　☞ want の破裂音 [t] が脱落しながら、弱化した to [ア] に連結。

❿ **want you**　　　ワント・ユー　　▶ ワンチュー
　☞ [t] + [j] の部分で音が混じり合い、[チュ] に近い音に変化する。

⓫ **in it**　　　イン・イット　　▶ イニッ(ト)
　☞ 2 語が連結。it 末尾の破裂音 [t] が脱落することもある。

⓬ **got to**　　　ガット・トゥー　　▶ ガッダ[ラ]
　☞ got に弱化した to [ア] が連結。連結部で [t] 音が弾音化する。

⓭ **little**　　　リトゥゥ　　▶ リドゥ[ル]ゥ
　☞ 破裂音 [t] が弾音化する。

⓮ **let me**　　　レット・ミー　　▶ レッ_ミー
　☞ let の破裂音 [t] が脱落する。

⓯ **front of**　　　フラント・アヴ　　▶ フラナ_
　☞ front 末尾の破裂音 [t] が脱落しつつ of に連結する。of の [v] 音も脱落。

Unit 9 超自然ドラマ
Supernatural Drama (Lost type)

Stage 1 穴埋めドラマ・リスニング

音声変化に注意してCDでドラマの音声を聴きながら空欄部分を埋めてみよう。CDのナチュラル音声での聴き取りが難しいときは、次のトラックに収録されたスロー音声で聴いてみよう。

● ● ● ● ● ●

A Recently I ① _____ _____ really weird dreams, you know?

B Sure, everybody does, right?

A Yeah, ② _____ _____ ... I'm not so sure they're just dreams.

B ③ _____ _____ might they be? Do you think they're telling you something about why we're here?

A I really ④ _____ know. ⑤ _____ you know that ridge of hills just beyond our encampment? You know how when we first got here somebody said they looked like the spine of a dragon or a dinosaur or something?

B Yeah, but it's not ⑥ _____ _____ for a ridge to look like that.

A Yeah, ⑦ _____ _____ my dream, they move; ⑧ _____ _____ like they're shaking themselves. Like a giant beast is slowly waking itself up.

B They're just dreams, Ben. That's all they are. Everybody's a ⑨ _____ freaked out now, ⑩ _____ _____ _____ mean ...

A But how about Clarke? Nobody has seen him for three days now. ⑪ _____ _____ he headed out towards those hills. And ⑫ _____ _____ _____ birds? ⑬ _____ _____ noticed ⑭ _____ they've been acting strangely ⑮ _____?

B Ben, we all need to stay calm. We need to keep our heads. Clarke told us he might be gone for a few days, you remember that, right?

A Karen, I'm scared. Something really evil is threatening us all. I can feel it. I'm SURE of it!

Stage 2 ドラマのシーン解説

日本語訳と、解説を参照しながら、ドラマの内容を確認しよう。そのあとで、Stage1の穴埋めに再チャレンジしてみよう。

A Recently I ① **get these** really weird dreams, you know?

最近、ものすごく奇妙な夢を見るんだ。

* weird「奇妙な」

B Sure, everybody does, right?

ええ、だれだって見るわよね?

A Yeah, ② **but these** ... I'm not so sure they're just dreams.

ああ、でも、その夢が…ただの夢なのかどうかわからないんだ。

超自然ドラマ 59

B ③ **What else** might they be? Do you think they're telling you something about why we're here?

ほかのなにかもしれないって言うの？ 私たちがここにいる理由について、夢があなたになにか伝えていると思ってるの？

* why we're here「私たちがここにいる理由」

A I really ④ **don't** know. ⑤ **But** you know that ridge of hills just beyond our encampment? You know how when we first got here somebody said they looked like the spine of a dragon or a dinosaur or something?

よくわからないんだ。でも、僕らの野営地のすぐ向こうの、あの山の尾根を知っているよね？ 僕らが最初にここにやってきたとき、だれかが言ってたんだよ。尾根がドラゴンや恐竜かなにかの背骨みたいに見えるってさ。

* ridge「尾根」　just beyond ...「…のすぐ向こうの」　encampment「野営地」　spine「背骨」
 ... or something「…かなにか」

B Yeah, but it's not ⑥ **that unusual** for a ridge to look like that.

ええ、でも尾根がそんな感じに見えるのは、それほど不思議なことじゃないわ。

* unusual「ふつうでない；異常な」

A Yeah, ⑦ **but in** my dream, they move; ⑧ **kind of** like they're shaking themselves. Like a giant beast is slowly waking itself up.

ああ、でも僕の夢では、尾根が動くんだよ…ある種、自分たちを揺らすようにね。巨大な獣がゆっくりと己の目覚めの準備を整えているみたいに。

* shake「揺らす；揺する」　beast「獣」　wake up「目を覚まさせる」

B They're just dreams, Ben. That's all they are. Everybody's a ⑨ **little** freaked out now, ⑩ **but that doesn't** mean ...

ただの夢よ、ベン。それだけのことよ。いまはみんなちょっとおかしくなっているのよ、で

もそれは…ってことじゃないけど…

* freaked out「パニックになって；おかしくなって」

Ⓐ But how about Clarke? Nobody has seen him for three days now. ⑪ **Right after** he headed out towards those hills. And ⑫ **how about the** birds? ⑬ **Haven't you** noticed ⑭ **that** they've been acting strangely ⑮ **lately**?

でも、クラークは？ もう3日も彼のことをだれも見ていないんだ。ちょうど彼があの山に向かってから。それに、鳥は？ 最近おかしな振る舞いなのに気づいてないのかい？

Ⓑ Ben, we all need to stay calm. We need to keep our heads. Clarke told us he might be gone for a few days, you remember that, right?

ベン、みんなが落ち着くことが必要なのよ。冷静になる必要があるの。クラークは数日帰ってこないかもしれないと言ったわ。覚えているでしょ？

* stay calm「落ち着いている」　keep one's head「冷静でいる」

Ⓐ Karen, I'm scared. Something really evil is threatening us all. I can feel it. I'm SURE of it!

カレン、僕は恐ろしいんだよ。なにかものすごく邪悪なものが、僕ら全員に迫っているんだ。感じるんだよ。確かに感じるんだよ！

* evil「邪悪な」　sure「確かな」

Stage 3 英文トランスクリプション

ドラマのシーン全体を英文の原稿で確認しながらCDで耳慣らししよう！ その上で、ドラマ・シーンの音声を聴きながら、まだできていない部分の穴埋めに再チャレンジしよう。

● ● ● ● ●

A Recently I ① **get these** really weird dreams, you know?

B Sure, everybody does, right?

A Yeah, ② **but these** … I'm not so sure they're just dreams.

B ③ **What else** might they be? Do you think they're telling you something about why we're here?

A I really ④ **don't** know. ⑤ **But** you know that ridge of hills just beyond our encampment? You know how when we first got here somebody said they looked like the spine of a dragon or a dinosaur or something?

B Yeah, but it's not ⑥ **that unusual** for a ridge to look like that.

A Yeah, ⑦ **but in** my dream, they move; ⑧ **kind of** like they're shaking themselves. Like a giant beast is slowly waking itself up.

B They're just dreams, Ben. That's all they are. Everybody's a ⑨ **little** freaked out now, ⑩ **but that doesn't** mean …

A But how about Clarke? Nobody has seen him for three days now. ⑪ **Right after** he headed out towards those hills. And ⑫ **how about the** birds? ⑬ **Haven't you** noticed ⑭ **that** they've been acting strangely ⑮ **lately**?

B Ben, we all need to stay calm. We need to keep our heads. Clarke told us he might be gone for a few days, you remember that, right?

A Karen, I'm scared. Something really evil is threatening us all. I can feel it. I'm SURE of it!

Stage 4 音声変化をチェック

まとめとして、穴埋め部分の音声変化の特徴を**スロー・スピード**と**ナチュラル・スピード**で確認しよう。下記に示したカタカナ表記で音声変化を確認して、もう一度ドラマを聴き直してみよう。発音変化のルールは適宜復習しよう。

❶ get these　　　　　　　　　ゲット・ズィーズ　　　　▶ ゲッ_ズィーズ
　☞ get の破裂音 [t] が脱落する。

❷ but these　　　　　　　　　バット・ズィーズ　　　　▶ バッ_ズィーズ
　☞ but の破裂音 [t] が脱落する。

❸ What else　　　　　　　　　ワット・エゥス　　　　　▶ ワッデ [レ] ゥス
　☞ 連結部で [t] 音が弾音化する。

❹ don't　　　　　　　　　　　ドウント　　　　　　　　▶ ドン_
　☞ 弱化して [ドン] という発音になる。

❺ But　　　　　　　　　　　　バット　　　　　　　　　▶ バッ_
　☞ 末尾の破裂音 [t] が脱落する。

❻ that unusual　　　　　　　　ザット・アンユージャゥ　▶ ザッダ [ラ] ンユージャゥ
　☞ 連結部で [t] 音が弾音化する。

❼ but in　　　　　　　　　　　バット・イン　　　　　　▶ バッディ [リ] ン
　☞ 連結部で [t] 音が弾音化する。

❽ kind of　　　　　　　　　　カインド・アヴ　　　　　▶ カインダヴ；カイナヴ
　☞ 2 語が連結する。kind の [d] 音が脱落しながら連結する場合もある。

❾ little　　　　　　　　　　　リトゥゥ　　　　　　　　▶ リドゥ [ル] ゥ
　☞ 破裂音 [t] が弾音化する。

❿ but that doesn't　　　　　　バット・ザット・ダズント　▶ バッ_ザッ_ダズン_
　☞ 3 語の末尾の破裂音 [t] が脱落する。

⓫ Right after　　　　　　　　ライト・アフター　　　　▶ ライダ [ラ] フター
　☞ 連結部で [t] 音が弾音化する。

⓬ how about the　　　　　　　ハウ・アバウト・ザ　　　▶ ハウ_バウッ_ザ
　☞ about から頭の [ə] 音や末尾の破裂音 [t] が脱落する。

⓭ Haven't you　　　　　　　　ハヴント・ユー　　　　　▶ ハヴンチュー
　☞ [t] + [j] の部分で音が混じり合い、[チュ] に近い音に変化する。

⓮ that　　　　　　　　　　　　ザット　　　　　　　　　▶ _アッ_
　☞ that が極端に弱化して [ə] 音のみが残ることがある。

⓯ lately　　　　　　　　　　　レイトゥリー　　　　　　▶ レイドゥ [ル] リー
　☞ 破裂音 [t] が弾音化する。

超自然ドラマ

Unit 10 オフィス・コメディー
Workplace Comedy (Ugly Betty type)

Stage 1 穴埋めドラマ・リスニング

音声変化に注意してCDでドラマの音声を聴きながら空欄部分を埋めてみよう。CDのナチュラル音声での聴き取りが難しいときは、次のトラックに収録されたスロー音声で聴いてみよう。

● ● ● ● ●

Ⓐ It's illegal to kill your boss, ① _____?

Ⓑ Uh, yeah, I'm ② _____ sure. In most states, anyway. Why does ③ _____ deserve to get whacked THIS time?

Ⓐ Well, for ④ _____, she blames me for every single thing ⑤ _____ _____ wrong here.

Ⓑ That's Natalie. We're her 'minions' after all. ⑥ _____ you're still a newbie, in her eyes.

Ⓐ ⑦ _____ _____ been here almost two years! I'm tired of being the office pin cushion!

Ⓑ Look, dealing with Natalie isn't easy. She's a ⑧ _____ freak, and most days we all hate her. ⑨ _____ _____ need to show a ⑩ _____ backbone, girl. You ⑪ _____ _____ push you around too much.

Ⓐ Hmmmm ... yeah, but standing up to her is a good way to get my tushie tossed out of here.

Ⓑ Not necessarily. Natalie's like a ... a bear. Or a shark. Or ...

A I think of her more as a black widow spider or a cobra, ⑫ _____.

B Yeah, maybe. Anyway, what I mean is that she senses fear. She treats you the way she does because she knows you won't ⑬ _____ _____.

A You're right. I ⑭ _____ _____ be more assertive.
I ⑮ _____ _____ _____ just push me around all the time.

B That's the spirit!

Stage 2 ドラマのシーン解説

日本語訳と、解説を参照しながら、ドラマの内容を確認しよう。そのあとで、Stage1の穴埋めに再チャレンジしてみよう。

A It's illegal to kill your boss, ① **right**?

ボスを殺すのは不法でしょ？

* illegal「不法な」

B Uh, yeah, I'm ② **pretty** sure. In most states, anyway. Why does ③ **Natalie** deserve to get whacked THIS time?

あー、そうだね、かなり確実だ。とにかくほとんどの州ではね。どうして今回、ナタリーは殺害するに値するんだい？

* get whacked「殺される」

オフィス・コメディー 65

A Well, for ④ **starters**, she blames me for every single thing ⑤ **that goes** wrong here.

そうですね、まず第一に、彼女はここでうまくいかなかったことは全部私のせいにするんですよ。

* for starters「まず」　blame「非難する」

B That's Natalie. We're her 'minions' after all. ⑥ **And** you're still a newbie, in her eyes.

それがナタリーだよ。結局、僕らは彼女の「家来」だからね。それに、君はまだ彼女から見れば、ひよっこだからさ。

* minion「家来；子分；手下」　newbie「新米；初心者」

A ⑦ **But I've** been here almost two years! I'm tired of being the office pin cushion!

でも、私はここにほぼ2年いるんですよ！ 私はオフィスの針山になるのはもう飽き飽きなんですから！

* pin cushion「針山」

B Look, dealing with Natalie isn't easy. She's a ⑧ **control** freak, and most days we all hate her. ⑨ **But you** need to show a ⑩ **little** backbone, girl. You ⑪ **let her** push you around too much.

あのね、ナタリーとうまくやるのはかんたんじゃないんだよ。彼女はなにからなにまで口出しするから、ほとんど毎日、僕らはみんな彼女のことが大っ嫌いさ。でも、君はもうちょっと意地を見せる必要があるんだよ、お嬢ちゃん。君は、あまりにも、彼女に好きにいびらせちゃってるよ。

* control freak「仕切り屋」あらゆることに口を出してコントロールしたがる人。
　backbone「気骨；勇気」　push around「いじめる；あごで使う；こき使う」

A Hmmmm ... yeah, but standing up to her is a good way to get my tushie tossed out of here.

うーーーん、ええ。でも彼女に反抗するのは、私をここから追い出すいい口実になるんです。

* stand up to ...「…に立ち向かう」　tushie「お尻」　toss out「放り出す」

B Not necessarily. Natalie's like a ... a bear. Or a shark. Or ...

必ずしもそうではないよ。ナタリーは、熊みたいなものさ。あるいはサメ。あるいは…

A I think of her more as a black widow spider or a cobra, ⑫ **actually**.

実際、私は彼女はもっとクロゴケグモとかコブラとかだと思ってるんです。

B Yeah, maybe. Anyway, what I mean is that she senses fear. She treats you the way she does because she knows you won't ⑬ **fight back**.

ああ、かもね。とにかく、僕が言いたいのは、彼女は恐怖を感知するんだよ。君が言い返してこないとわかっているから、彼女はあのやり方で君を扱うのさ。

* sense「感じる；認識する；感知する」　fight back「抵抗する；反撃する」

A You're right. I ⑭ **need to** be more assertive. I ⑮ **can't let her** just push me around all the time.

そのとおりです。もっとはっきり言わなくちゃです。いつもいつも、彼女にいびられ放題になってばかりはいられないんだから。

* assertive「正当に意見を主張する；はっきりと意見を述べる」

B That's the spirit!

その意気だよ！

* spirit「気迫；気力」

Stage 3　英文トランスクリプション

ドラマのシーン全体を英文の原稿で確認しながらCDで耳慣らししよう！　その上で、ドラマ・シーンの音声を聴きながら、まだできていない部分の穴埋めに再チャレンジしよう。

● ● ● ● ● ●

A It's illegal to kill your boss, ① **right**?

B Uh, yeah, I'm ② **pretty** sure. In most states, anyway. Why does ③ **Natalie** deserve to get whacked THIS time?

A Well, for ④ **starters**, she blames me for every single thing ⑤ **that goes** wrong here.

B That's Natalie. We're her 'minions' after all. ⑥ **And** you're still a newbie, in her eyes.

A ⑦ **But I've** been here almost two years! I'm tired of being the office pin cushion!

B Look, dealing with Natalie isn't easy. She's a ⑧ **control** freak, and most days we all hate her. ⑨ **But you** need to show a ⑩ **little** backbone, girl. You ⑪ **let her** push you around too much.

A Hmmmm ... yeah, but standing up to her is a good way to get my tushie tossed out of here.

B Not necessarily. Natalie's like a ... a bear. Or a shark. Or ...

A I think of her more as a black widow spider or a cobra, ⑫ **actually**.

B Yeah, maybe. Anyway, what I mean is that she senses fear. She treats you the way she does because she knows you won't ⑬ **fight back**.

A You're right. I ⑭ **need to** be more assertive. I ⑮ **can't let her** just push me around all the time.

B That's the spirit!

68

Stage 4 音声変化をチェック

CD 1-31

まとめとして、穴埋め部分の音声変化の特徴を**スロー・スピード**と**ナチュラル・スピード**で確認しよう。下記に示したカタカナ表記で音声変化を確認して、もう一度ドラマを聴き直してみよう。発音変化のルールは適宜復習しよう。

❶ right　　　　　　　　　　ライト　　　　　　　▶ ライッ＿
☞ right 末尾の破裂音 [t] が脱落する。

❷ pretty　　　　　　　　　　プリティー　　　　　▶ プリディ [リ] ー
☞ 破裂音 [t] が弾音化する。

❸ Natalie　　　　　　　　　ナタリー　　　　　　▶ ナダ [ラ] リー
☞ 破裂音 [t] が弾音化する。

❹ starters　　　　　　　　　スターターズ　　　　▶ スターダ [ラ] ーズ
☞ 破裂音 [t] が弾音化する。

❺ that goes　　　　　　　　ザット・ゴウズ　　　▶ ザッ＿ゴウズ
☞ that 末尾の破裂音 [t] が脱落する。

❻ And　　　　　　　　　　　アンド　　　　　　　▶ アン＿
☞ 末尾の破裂音 [d] が脱落する。

❼ But I've　　　　　　　　 バット・アイヴ　　　▶ バッダ [ラ] イヴ
☞ 2語が連結。連結部で破裂音 [t] が弾音化する。

❽ control　　　　　　　　　カントゥローゥ　　　▶ カンチュローゥ
☞ [tr] 部分の [t] 音が [チュ] に近い音に変化する。

❾ But you　　　　　　　　　バット・ユー　　　　▶ バッ＿ユー
☞ But 末尾の破裂音 [t] が脱落する。

❿ little　　　　　　　　　　リトゥゥ　　　　　　▶ リドゥ [ル] ゥ
☞ 破裂音 [t] が弾音化する。

⓫ let her　　　　　　　　　レット・ハー　　　　▶ レッダ [ラ] ー
☞ let に弱化した her [アー] が連結。連結部で [t] 音が弾音化する。

⓬ actually　　　　　　　　 アクチュアリー　　　▶ アクシュアリー
☞ 破裂音 [t] が脱落する。

⓭ fight back　　　　　　　 ファイト・バック　　▶ ファイッ＿バック
☞ fight 末尾の破裂音 [t] が脱落する。

⓮ need to　　　　　　　　　ニード・トゥー　　　▶ ニーッ＿トゥー
☞ need 末尾の破裂音 [d] が脱落する。

⓯ can't let her　　　　　　キャント・レット・ハー　▶ キャン＿レッダ [ラ] ー
☞ can't 末尾の破裂音 [t] が脱落。let に弱化した her [アー] が連結。連結部で [t] 音が弾音化する。

オフィス・コメディー　69

Unit 11 逃亡者ドラマ
Escapee Drama (Prison Break type)

Stage 1 穴埋めドラマ・リスニング

音声変化に注意してCDでドラマの音声を聴きながら空欄部分を埋めてみよう。CDのナチュラル音声での聴き取りが難しいときは、次のトラックに収録されたスロー音声で聴いてみよう。

● ● ● ● ● ●

A How long you been on the run?

B I ① _____ _____ know, six months maybe. What day ② _____ _____ ?

A It's June something. I think the 26th.

B I just know ③ _____ _____ cold when I ④ _____ _____. I don't feel like doing the math.

A How long you figure you can last? How long before ⑤ _____ _____ you down?

B Look, all I know is I'm gonna clear my name. However long that takes. ⑥ _____ I'm gonna ⑦ _____ _____ some payback from the dudes that set me up.

A Is there anyone you can trust ⑧ _____ _____ outside?

B I got nobody, man. Trusting's what ⑨ _____ _____ in the can, ⑩ _____ _____ don't intend to go back.

A Look, Adam, I don't know ⑪ _____ _____ want from me.

70

I mean I don't ⑫ _____ _____ get mixed up in all this shit.

B You ⑬ _____ mixed up in nothing. You just stay cool, and in two or three days I'll be gone. You'll never see me again.

A Look, ⑭ _____ _____ _____ wrong. I mean I wish I could help you, but ...

B It's okay, Jill. You were always good to my brother, and I ⑮ _____ that. Just give me two days, that's the only thing I'll ever ask you for.

Stage 2 ドラマのシーン解説

日本語訳と、解説を参照しながら、ドラマの内容を確認しよう。そのあとで、Stage1の穴埋めに再チャレンジしてみよう。

A How long you been on the run?

どのくらい逃亡生活をしているの？

* on the run「逃亡して；逃走中の」

B I ① **don't even** know, six months maybe. What day ② **is it**?

それすらわからないんだ、おそらく6カ月くらい。今日は何日なんだ？

A It's June something. I think the 26th.

6月何日かよ。26日だと思う。

逃亡者ドラマ 71

B I just know ③ **it was** cold when I ④ **broke out**. I don't feel like doing the math.

脱獄したときに、寒かったのだけはわかるが、計算をする気分じゃないんだ。

✳ break out (of prison)「脱獄する」

A How long you figure you can last? How long before ⑤ **it wears** you down?

どのくらい持ちこたえられると思うの？ 逃亡生活に疲れ切っちゃうまで、どのくらいがんばれる？

✳ figure「思う；考える；計算する」 last「持ちこたえる」 wear down「根負けさせる；粘って勝つ」

B Look, all I know is I'm gonna clear my name. However long that takes. ⑥ **And** I'm gonna ⑦ **get me** some payback from the dudes that set me up.

あのな、俺にわかっているのは、自分の汚名をそそぐんだってことだけなんだよ。どれほど長い時間がかかってもだ。そして、俺をはめた奴に仕返しをするのさ。

✳ clear one's name「汚名を返上する」 however ...「どんなに…だとしても」
　payback「仕返し；復讐」 dude「奴；野郎」 set ... up「…を（罠などに）はめる」

A Is there anyone you can trust ⑧ **on the** outside?

刑務所の外には、だれか信頼できる人はいるの？

✳ outside「娑婆（しゃば）」

B I got nobody, man. Trusting's what ⑨ **put me** in the can, ⑩ **and I** don't intend to go back.

だれもいないさ。信頼することでブタ箱に放り込まれたんだ。そして、もう戻るつもりはないね。

✳ put ... in the can「…を刑務所に入れる」 intend to ...「…するつもりだ」

A Look, Adam, I don't know ⑪ **what you** want from me. I mean I don't ⑫ **want to** get mixed up in all this shit.

あのね、アダム。あなたが私になにをしてほしいのかわからないわ。つまりね、私はこのごたごたに巻き込まれたくはないの。

* get mixed up in ... 「…に巻き込まれる；関わる」 shit 「くだらない物事；クソ」

B You ⑬ **ain't** mixed up in nothing. You just stay cool, and in two or three days I'll be gone. You'll never see me again.

君はなんにも巻き込まれたりはしないよ。ただ静かにしていれば、2、3日で俺はいなくなる。二度と俺の顔を見ることもない。

* stay cool 「落ち着いている」

A Look, ⑭ **don't get me** wrong. I mean I wish I could help you, but ...

あのね、誤解しないでほしいの。つまり、できればあなたの助けになりたいのよ、でもね…

* get someone wrong 「…の言動を取り違える；誤解する」

B It's okay, Jill. You were always good to my brother, and I ⑮ **appreciate** that. Just give me two days, that's the only thing I'll ever ask you for.

いいんだ、ジル。君は、いつも俺の兄弟に優しくしてくれたし、感謝してるよ。2日だけ俺にくれよ、俺が君に頼みたいのは、とにかくそれだけなんだ。

* appreciate 「感謝する」

逃亡者ドラマ

Stage 3 英文トランスクリプション

ドラマのシーン全体を英文の原稿で確認しながらCDで耳慣らししよう！ その上で、ドラマ・シーンの音声を聴きながら、まだできていない部分の穴埋めに再チャレンジしよう。

・・・・・・

A How long you been on the run?

B I ① **don't even** know, six months maybe. What day ② **is it**?

A It's June something. I think the 26th.

B I just know ③ **it was** cold when I ④ **broke out**. I don't feel like doing the math.

A How long you figure you can last? How long before ⑤ **it wears** you down?

B Look, all I know is I'm gonna clear my name. However long that takes. ⑥ **And** I'm gonna ⑦ **get me** some payback from the dudes that set me up.

A Is there anyone you can trust ⑧ **on the** outside?

B I got nobody, man. Trusting's what ⑨ **put me** in the can, ⑩ **and I** don't intend to go back.

A Look, Adam, I don't know ⑪ **what you** want from me. I mean I don't ⑫ **want to** get mixed up in all this shit.

B You ⑬ **ain't** mixed up in nothing. You just stay cool, and in two or three days I'll be gone. You'll never see me again.

A Look, ⑭ **don't get me** wrong. I mean I wish I could help you, but …

B It's okay, Jill. You were always good to my brother, and I ⑮ **appreciate** that. Just give me two days, that's the only thing I'll ever ask you for.

Stage 4 音声変化をチェック

まとめとして、穴埋め部分の音声変化の特徴を**スロー・スピード**と**ナチュラル・スピード**で確認しよう。下記に示したカタカナ表記で音声変化を確認して、もう一度ドラマを聴き直してみよう。発音変化のルールは適宜復習しよう。

❶ **don't even** 　　　　ドウント・イーヴン 　　▶ ドニーヴン
　☞ don't は弱化。don't 末尾の破裂音 [t] が脱落しつつ、2 語が連結する。

❷ **is it** 　　　　　　　イズ・イット 　　　　　▶ イズィッ＿
　☞ 2 語が連結。it 末尾の破裂音 [t] が脱落する。

❸ **it was** 　　　　　　イット・ワズ 　　　　　▶ イッ＿ワズ
　☞ it 末尾の破裂音 [t] が脱落する。

❹ **broke out** 　　　　 ブロウク・アウト 　　　　▶ ブロウクアウッ＿
　☞ out 末尾の破裂音 [t] が脱落する。

❺ **it wears** 　　　　　イット・ウェアーズ 　　　▶ イッ＿ウェアーズ
　☞ it 末尾の破裂音 [t] が脱落する。

❻ **And** 　　　　　　　アンド 　　　　　　　　▶ アン＿
　☞ And 末尾の破裂音 [d] が脱落する。

❼ **get me** 　　　　　　ゲット・ミー 　　　　　▶ ゲッ＿ミー
　☞ get 末尾の破裂音 [t] が脱落する。

❽ **on the** 　　　　　　オン・ズィ 　　　　　　▶ オニ
　☞ [n] + [ð] が [n] 音に変化する。

❾ **put me** 　　　　　　プット・ミー 　　　　　▶ プッ＿ミー
　☞ put 末尾の破裂音 [t] が脱落する。

❿ **and I** 　　　　　　アンド・アイ 　　　　　▶ アナイ
　☞ and 末尾の破裂音 [d] が脱落しつつ、I に連結する。

⓫ **what you** 　　　　　ワット・ユー 　　　　　▶ ワッチュー
　☞ [t] + [j] の部分で音が混じり合い、[チュ] に近い音に変化する。

⓬ **want to** 　　　　　　ワント・トゥー 　　　　▶ ワナ
　☞ want 末尾の破裂音 [t] が脱落しつつ、弱化した to [ア] に連結する。

⓭ **ain't** 　　　　　　 エイント 　　　　　　　▶ エイン＿
　☞ ain't 末尾の破裂音 [t] が脱落する。

⓮ **don't get me** 　　　ドウント・ゲット・ミー 　▶ ドン＿ゲッ＿ミー
　☞ don't は弱化。don't や get 末尾の破裂音 [t] が脱落する。

⓯ **appreciate** 　　　　アプリーシェイト 　　　　▶ アプリーシェイッ＿
　☞ 末尾の破裂音 [t] が脱落する。

逃亡者ドラマ　75

Unit 12 青春ドラマ
Teenager Drama (Glee type)

Stage 1 穴埋めドラマ・リスニング

音声変化に注意してCDでドラマの音声を聴きながら空欄部分を埋めてみよう。CDのナチュラル音声での聴き取りが難しいときは、次のトラックに収録されたスロー音声で聴いてみよう。

● ● ● ● ●

A ① _____ _____ _____ like for you when you came
② _____ _____ your parents?

B My mom was so funny! She was like, oh honey, I knew all along!

A Really? ③ _____ was she cool ④ _____ _____ ?

B Yeah, my mom's great. She's like my best friend!

A Wow, you're lucky. How ⑤ _____ _____ dad?

B My dad? He has, like, a gift for ⑥ _____ _____ . He ⑦ _____ explaining how ⑧ _____ _____ was ⑨ _____ , he was too busy at work to play catch with me!

A Ha ha, no WAY! He thinks you became gay because he ⑩ _____ play catch with you?

B Who knows? He's weird. But yeah, he kind of blamed himself at first. ⑪ _____ _____ ⑫ _____ now. I think he just kind of accepts it.

A I'm dreading telling my parents. They're not like yours. They're like, "God intended men and women for each other blah blah blah."

B Oh, god. Does anyone in your family know?

A I ⑬ _____ know. My brother ⑭ _____ suspect. The thing is, I've always been the black sheep of my family, ⑮_____ _____ just adds to it.

B It's okay. Families should always be able to lend support. If they can't, it's THEIR problem, not yours.

Stage 2 ドラマのシーン解説

日本語訳と、解説を参照しながら、ドラマの内容を確認しよう。そのあとで、Stage1の穴埋めに再チャレンジしてみよう。

A ① **What was it** like for you when you came ② **out to** your parents?

ご両親に告白したときは、どんな気持ちだったの？

＊ come out「秘密を明かす；同性愛者であると告げる」

B My mom was so funny! She was like, oh honey, I knew all along!

母はおもしろかったよ！ 彼女は、あら、あなた、私はずっとお見通しだったわよ、って感じだったの！

＊ all along「ずっと」

青春ドラマ 77

A Really? ③ **And** was she cool ④ **with it**?

そうなの？ で、お母さんは大丈夫だったの？

B Yeah, my mom's great. She's like my best friend!

ええ、母はすばらしいの。私の親友みたいなのよ！

A Wow, you're lucky. How ⑤ **about your** dad?

へえ、あなたラッキーね。お父さんはどうだったの？

B My dad? He has, like, a gift for ⑥ **non sequiturs**. He ⑦ **started** explaining how ⑧ **when I** was ⑨ **little**, he was too busy at work to play catch with me!

父さん？ 父はね、無理矢理おかしな結論を導く才能があるのよ。私が小さかったときに、仕事で忙しくて私とキャッチボールができなかったことを弁明し始めちゃって！

＊ gift「才能」　non sequitur「無理な結論；不合理な推論」

A Ha ha, no WAY! He thinks you became gay because he ⑩ **didn't** play catch with you?

ハハ、あり得ないわ！ お父さんは、自分があなたとキャッチボールをしなかったから、あなたがゲイになったと思ってるの？

B Who knows? He's weird. But yeah, he kind of blamed himself at first. ⑪ **But it's** ⑫ **better** now. I think he just kind of accepts it.

さあねえ。父は変わってるのよ。でも、うん、最初は、なんだか自分自身を責めていたわ。いまはだいぶよくなったけど。なんとなく、事実を納得したんだと思う。

＊ blame oneself「自分自身を責める」　accept「受け入れる」

A I'm dreading telling my parents. They're not like yours. They're like, "God intended men and women for each other blah blah blah."

私は両親に告げるのがものすごく恐いの。 おたくの両親とは違うのよ。うちの両親はね「神は男女を互いのために作りたもうたとかなんとか…」って感じなの。

* dread「ひどく恐れる；心配する」　intend A for B「AをBのために予定・意図する」

B Oh, god. Does anyone in your family know?

ああ、なんてことなの。あなたのご家族で知ってる人はいるの？

A I ⑬ **don't** know. My brother ⑭ **might** suspect. The thing is, I've always been the black sheep of my family, ⑮ **and this** just adds to it.

さあ。兄はうすうす感じているのかも。問題はね、私はいつも家族の厄介者だったの、それで、この件がさらにややこしくなるのよ。

* suspect「怪しいと思う；うすうす感じる；疑う」　black sheep「厄介者；面汚し；異端者」
　add to ...「…にさらに影響を加える」

B It's okay. Families should always be able to lend support. If they can't, it's THEIR problem, not yours.

大丈夫よ。家族はいつだって支えてくれるべきなの。もし、それができない家族なら、それは彼らの問題で、あなたのせいではないのよ。

* lend support「支えの手を差し出す」

Stage 3 英文トランスクリプション

ドラマのシーン全体を英文の原稿で確認しながらCDで耳慣らししよう！ その上で、ドラマ・シーンの音声を聴きながら、まだできていない部分の穴埋めに再チャレンジしよう。

• • • • • •

A ① **What was it** like for you when you came ② **out to** your parents?

B My mom was so funny! She was like, oh honey, I knew all along!

A Really? ③ **And** was she cool ④ **with it**?

B Yeah, my mom's great. She's like my best friend!

A Wow, you're lucky. How ⑤ **about your** dad?

B My dad? He has, like, a gift for ⑥ **non sequiturs**. He ⑦ **started** explaining how ⑧ **when I** was ⑨ **little**, he was too busy at work to play catch with me!

A Ha ha, no WAY! He thinks you became gay because he ⑩ **didn't** play catch with you?

B Who knows? He's weird. But yeah, he kind of blamed himself at first. ⑪ **But it's** ⑫ **better** now. I think he just kind of accepts it.

A I'm dreading telling my parents. They're not like yours. They're like, "God intended men and women for each other blah blah blah."

B Oh, god. Does anyone in your family know?

A I ⑬ **don't** know. My brother ⑭ **might** suspect. The thing is, I've always been the black sheep of my family, ⑮ **and this** just adds to it.

B It's okay. Families should always be able to lend support. If they can't, it's THEIR problem, not yours.

80

Stage 4 音声変化をチェック

まとめとして、穴埋め部分の音声変化の特徴を**スロー・スピード**と**ナチュラル・スピード**で確認しよう。下記に示したカタカナ表記で音声変化を確認して、もう一度ドラマを聴き直してみよう。発音変化のルールは適宜復習しよう。

❶ What was it　　　ワット・ワズ・イット　　　▶ ワッ＿ワズィッ＿
☞ What 末尾の破裂音 [t] が脱落する。was it は連結。it 末尾の破裂音 [t] も脱落。

❷ out to　　　アウト・トゥー　　　▶ アウッ＿トゥー
☞ out 末尾の破裂音 [t] が脱落する。

❸ And　　　アンド　　　▶ アン＿
☞ And 末尾の破裂音 [d] が脱落する。

❹ with it　　　ウィズ・イット　　　▶ ウィズィッ＿
☞ 2語が連結する。it 末尾の破裂音 [t] は脱落する。

❺ about your　　　アバウト・ユア　　　▶ アバウチュア
☞ 連結部で [t] + [j] の部分で音が混じり合い、[チュ] に近い音に変化する。

❻ non sequiturs　　　ノン・セクァターズ　　　▶ ノンセクァダ [ラ] ーズ
☞ 破裂音 [t] が弾音化する。

❼ started　　　スターティッド　　　▶ スターディ [リ] ッド
☞ 破裂音 [t] が弾音化する。

❽ when I　　　ウェン・アイ　　　▶ ウェナイ
☞ 2語が連結する。

❾ little　　　リトゥゥ　　　▶ リドゥ [ル] ゥ
☞ 破裂音 [t] が弾音化する。

❿ didn't　　　ディドゥント　　　▶ ディドゥン＿
☞ 末尾の破裂音 [t] が脱落する。

⓫ But it's　　　バット・イッツ　　　▶ バッディ [リ] ッツ
☞ 2語が連結。連結部で破裂音 [t] が弾音化する。

⓬ better　　　ベター　　　▶ ベダ [ラ] ー
☞ 破裂音 [t] が弾音化する。

⓭ don't　　　ドウント　　　▶ ドン＿
☞ don't は弱化。末尾の破裂音 [t] が脱落する。

⓮ might　　　マイト　　　▶ マイッ＿
☞ 末尾の破裂音 [t] が脱落する。

⓯ and this　　　アンド・ズィス　　　▶ アン＿ズィス
☞ and 末尾の破裂音 [d] が脱落する。

Unit 13 警察ドラマ
Police Drama (Cops type)

Stage 1 穴埋めドラマ・リスニング

音声変化に注意してCDでドラマの音声を聴きながら空欄部分を埋めてみよう。CDのナチュラル音声での聴き取りが難しいときは、次のトラックに収録されたスロー音声で聴いてみよう。

● ● ● ● ● ●

A This is Detective Reynolds. I'm responding to an APB ① _____ _____ possible robbery in progress on Essex Avenue.

B Copy that, Charlie. ② _____ _____ _____ got?

A Just arriving on the scene now … Holy shit!

B Charlie? Charlie, do you copy?

A Yes! There is a major heist operation in progress! An armored ③ _____ _____ on the scene. Do you read?

B We read you. Charlie, you're the first responder. We recommend you await backup.

A Hell yes, ④ _____ _____ some backup! This looks like a military operation!

B ⑤ _____ cars are now ⑥ _____ _____ way to you from the north and the southeast. Shall we ⑦ _____ _____ chopper unit?

A Yeah, ⑧ _____ _____ _____ chopper. I just ⑨ _____ my first sight of ⑩ _____ _____ _____ perps. These guys are heavily armed.

82

B Any guess ⑪ _____ how many there are?

A Not yet; the rest appear ⑫ _____ _____ inside. This guy has paramilitary ⑬ _____.

B How about the driver of the vehicle?

A I ⑭ _____ _____ _____ good look. When are those cars gonna get here?

B Maybe half a minute, maybe less.

A I hear them coming. Make sure that chopper gets here. THIS IS DETECTIVE REYNOLDS OF THE MIAMI POLICE DEPARTMENT. CEASE AND DESIST YOUR ⑮ _____ IMMEDIATELY!

Stage 2 ドラマのシーン解説

日本語訳と、解説を参照しながら、ドラマの内容を確認しよう。そのあとで、Stage1の穴埋めに再チャレンジしてみよう。

A This is Detective Reynolds. I'm responding to an APB ① **on a** possible robbery in progress on Essex Avenue.

こちら、レイノルズ刑事。エセックス・アヴァニューで現在進行中の強盗と思われる事件に関する緊急手配に対応しています。

B Copy that, Charlie. ② **What have you** got?

了解、チャーリー。なにをつかんだ？

A Just arriving on the scene now … Holy shit!

ちょうど、現場に到着するところで…なんてこった！

警察ドラマ 83

B Charlie? Charlie, do you copy?

チャーリー? チャーリー、聞こえているか?

A Yes! There is a major heist operation in progress! An armored ③ **vehicle is** on the scene. Do you read?

はい! 大規模な強盗事件が進行中です! 武装した車両が現場にあります。聞こえますか?

* heist「強盗;盗み」 operation「活動」 armed「武装した」
read「(無線通信などで) 聴き取る;理解する」

B We read you. Charlie, you're the first responder. We recommend you await backup.

聞こえている。チャーリー、君が最初の対応をしているが、支援を待つことをすすめる。

* await backup「支援を待つ」

A Hell yes, ④ **get me** some backup! This looks like a military operation!

もちろんです、支援を送ってください! まるでこれは、軍事作戦みたいです!

* military operation「軍事行動」

B ⑤ **Patrol** cars are now ⑥ **making their** way to you from the north and the southeast. Shall we ⑦ **send a** chopper unit?

北と南東から、パトカーが君のもとへ向かっている。ヘリコプター部隊を送ろうか?

* chopper unit「ヘリコプター部隊」

A Yeah, ⑧ **get us a** chopper. I just ⑨ **got** my first sight of ⑩ **one of the** perps. These guys are heavily armed.

ええ、ヘリを送ってください。いま、犯人のひとりをはじめて目視しました。奴らは重武装し

ています。

* perp「犯人」 heavily armed「重武装した」

Ⓑ Any guess ⑪ **about** how many there are?

人数についての推測はできるか？

Ⓐ Not yet; the rest appear ⑫ **to be** inside. This guy has paramilitary ⑬ **outfitting**.

いいえ、まだ。残りは中にいる様子です。この人物は民兵のような装備です。

* paramilitary outfitting「準軍事的な装備」

Ⓑ How about the driver of the vehicle?

車両のドライバーはどうか？

Ⓐ I ⑭ **can't get a** good look. When are those cars gonna get here?

よく見えません。支援のパトカーはいつ到着しますか？

Ⓑ Maybe half a minute, maybe less.

おそらく 30 秒か、もっと早いだろう。

Ⓐ I hear them coming. Make sure that chopper gets here. THIS IS DETECTIVE REYNOLDS OF THE MIAMI POLICE DEPARTMENT. CEASE AND DESIST YOUR ⑮ **ACTIVITIES** IMMEDIATELY!

やってくる音が聞こえます。確実にこちらにヘリを送ってください。「こちら、マイアミ警察のレイノルズ刑事だ。行動を即刻、停止しなさい！」

* cease and desist ...「…を停止する」

Stage 3 英文トランスクリプション

ドラマのシーン全体を英文の原稿で確認しながらCDで耳慣らししよう！ その上で、ドラマ・シーンの音声を聴きながら、まだできていない部分の穴埋めに再チャレンジしよう。

● ● ● ● ● ●

A This is Detective Reynolds. I'm responding to an APB ① **on a** possible robbery in progress on Essex Avenue.

B Copy that, Charlie. ② **What have you** got?

A Just arriving on the scene now ... Holy shit!

B Charlie? Charlie, do you copy?

A Yes! There is a major heist operation in progress! An armored ③ **vehicle is** on the scene. Do you read?

B We read you. Charlie, you're the first responder. We recommend you await backup.

A Hell yes, ④ **get me** some backup! This looks like a military operation!

B ⑤ **Patrol** cars are now ⑥ **making their** way to you from the north and the southeast. Shall we ⑦ **send a** chopper unit?

A Yeah, ⑧ **get us a** chopper. I just ⑨ **got** my first sight of ⑩ **one of the** perps. These guys are heavily armed.

B Any guess ⑪ **about** how many there are?

A Not yet; the rest appear ⑫ **to be** inside. This guy has paramilitary ⑬ **outfitting**.

B How about the driver of the vehicle?

A I ⑭ **can't get a** good look. When are those cars gonna get here?

B Maybe half a minute, maybe less.

A I hear them coming. Make sure that chopper gets here. THIS IS DETECTIVE REYNOLDS OF THE MIAMI POLICE DEPARTMENT. CEASE AND DESIST YOUR ⑮ **ACTIVITIES** IMMEDIATELY!

Stage 4 音声変化をチェック

まとめとして、穴埋め部分の音声変化の特徴を**スロー・スピード**と**ナチュラル・スピード**で確認しよう。下記に示したカタカナ表記で音声変化を確認して、もう一度ドラマを聴き直してみよう。発音変化のルールは適宜復習しよう。

❶ on a   オン・ア   ▶ オナ
☞ 2語が連結する。

❷ What have you   ワット・ハヴ・ユー   ▶ ワッダ [ラ] ヴユ
☞ have you は弱化して [ァヴユ] と発話される。What と have の連結部で破裂音 [t] が弾音化する。

❸ vehicle is   ヴィアクゥ・イズ   ▶ ヴィアクゥズ
☞ 短縮された vehicle's の発音になる場合がある。

❹ get me   ゲット・ミー   ▶ ゲッ＿ミー
☞ get 末尾の破裂音 [t] が脱落する。

❺ Patrol   パトゥローゥ   ▶ パチュローゥ
☞ [tr] 部分の [t] 音が [チュ] に近い音に変化する。

❻ making their   メイキング・ゼア   ▶ メイキネア
☞ making の破裂音 [g] が脱落しつつ、2語が連結。連結部で [n] + [ð] が [n] 音に変化する。

❼ send a   センド・ア   ▶ センダ
☞ 2語が連結する。

❽ get us a   ゲット・アス・ア   ▶ ゲッダ [ラ] サ
☞ 3語が連結する。get us の連結部で破裂音 [t] が弾音化する。

❾ got   ガット   ▶ ガッ＿
☞ 末尾の破裂音 [t] が脱落する。

❿ one of the   ワン・アヴ・ザ   ▶ ワナ＿ザ
☞ one of が連結。of 末尾の [v] 音が脱落する。

⓫ about   アバウト   ▶ ＿ッバウッ＿
☞ 弱化して、頭の [ə] 音や末尾の破裂音 [t] が脱落する。

⓬ to be   トゥー・ビー   ▶ ドゥ [ル] ービー
☞ to の破裂音 [t] が弾音化する。

⓭ outfitting   アウトフィッティング   ▶ アウ (ト) フィッディ [リ] ン＿
☞ out- の [t] 音の脱落や、-fitting の [t] 音の弾音化、[g] 音の脱落が起こる。

⓮ can't get a   キャーント・ゲット・ア   ▶ キャーン＿ゲッダ [ラ]
☞ can't 末尾の [t] 音が脱落。get a の連結部で破裂音 [t] の弾音化が起こる。

⓯ ACTIVITIES   アクティヴィティーズ   ▶ アクティヴィディ [リ] ーズ
☞ 2番目の破裂音 [t] が弾音化する。

Unit 14 高校生ドラマ
High School Drama (Beverly Hills 90210 type)

Stage 1 穴埋めドラマ・リスニング

音声変化に注意してCDでドラマの音声を聴きながら空欄部分を埋めてみよう。CDのナチュラル音声での聴き取りが難しいときは、次のトラックに収録されたスロー音声で聴いてみよう。

● ● ● ● ●

A Hey, ① _____ _____ that girl ② _____ _____ walked by? I haven't seen her before. Did she just transfer here?

B Oh, yeah. Natalie. I suppose you think she's super hot, right? Like every other guy?

A Well, yeah, she is ③ _____ hot. ④ _____ _____ like a model or ⑤ _____?

B Yeah, but she's gross. Those boobs are ⑥ _____ fake. I think she had ⑦ _____ _____ nose job or something too.

A ⑧ _____ _____ sounds like a bunch of gossip! How do you know she ⑨ _____ _____ boob job?

B It's so, like, obvious! Anyway, half the guys have already ⑩ _____ _____ _____, so you'll have to ⑪ _____ _____ line, loverboy.

A Who said anything about hitting ⑫ _____ _____? I just asked ⑬ _____ _____.

88

B I saw the way you checked her out, though. You're such a douche sometimes, Vinnie.

A Better cool the jealousy, Sam. That shade of green clashes with your mascara.

B Oh, shut up. Why should I be jealous? If you ⑭ _____ _____ be shot down by Miss Fakey Boobs, be my guest.

A Wow, somebody needs to seriously chill. ⑮ _____ Sammy's no longer the center of attention, and it's killing her.

Stage 2 ドラマのシーン解説

日本語訳と、解説を参照しながら、ドラマの内容を確認しよう。そのあとで、Stage1の穴埋めに再チャレンジしてみよう。

A Hey, ① **who was** that girl ② **that just** walked by? I haven't seen her before. Did she just transfer here?

あのさ、さっき通り過ぎた女子ってだれだったの？ これまで見たことないんだけど。ここに転校してきたばかりなのかな？

＊ transfer「転校する」

B Oh, yeah. Natalie. I suppose you think she's super hot, right? Like every other guy?

ああ、そうよ。ナタリー。彼女のこと超イケてると思ってるんでしょ？ ほかの男子と同じよね？

高校生ドラマ 89

Ⓐ Well, yeah, she is ③ **pretty** hot. ④ **Is she** like a model or ⑤ **something**?

うーん、そうだね、彼女、かなりイケてる。モデルとかそんなのかな?

Ⓑ Yeah, but she's gross. Those boobs are ⑥ **totally** fake. I think she had ⑦ **like a** nose job or something too.

ええ、でも彼女、気持ち悪いの。おっぱいが完全な偽物なのよ。鼻の整形とかもやってるんだと思うわ。

* gross「気味の悪い；ぞっとする」 nose job「鼻の整形手術」

Ⓐ ⑧ **That just** sounds like a bunch of gossip! How do you know she ⑨ **had a** boob job?

それって、でたらめっぽいよね! どうして彼女が胸の整形をしてるってわかるんだい?

* gossip「うわさ話；陰口」

Ⓑ It's so, like, obvious! Anyway, half the guys have already ⑩ **hit on her**, so you'll have to ⑪ **get in** line, loverboy.

すごく、あのね、見え見えなのよ! とにかく、男子の半分は、もう彼女に言い寄ったって。だから、あなたも列に加わらなきゃね、色男さん。

* hit on ...「…に言い寄る」 loverboy「色男；美男子」

Ⓐ Who said anything about hitting ⑫ **on her**? I just asked ⑬ **about her**.

だれが彼女に言い寄るなんて話をしたんだよ? 僕は彼女のことをたずねただけだよ。

Ⓑ I saw the way you checked her out, though. You're such a douche sometimes, Vinnie.

90

でも、私、あなたが彼女をチェックしてた様子を見てたわ。あなた、たまにすごくウザいのよね、ビニー。

* douche「(女性をいやらしい目で見る) ウザい奴」

A Better cool the jealousy, Sam. That shade of green clashes with your mascara.

ヤキモチはやめろよ、サム。 嫉妬の緑の色合いは、君のマスカラには合わないよ。

* shade「色合い；ニュアンス」 green「緑」緑色は嫉妬を象徴する色。
  clash with ...「…に合わない；…と衝突する」

B Oh, shut up. Why should I be jealous? If you ⑭ **want to** be shot down by Miss Fakey Boobs, be my guest.

あー、黙りなさい。なんで私がヤキモチなんか妬くのよ？ あなたが、ミス偽おっぱいさんに振られたいのなら、どうぞご自由に。

* be shot down「拒絶される；振られる」 Be my guest.「どうぞご自由に；ご遠慮なく」

A Wow, somebody needs to seriously chill. ⑮ **Little** Sammy's no longer the center of attention, and it's killing her.

へえ、だれかさん、ホントに頭を冷やさないとね。サミーちゃんはもう注目の的じゃなくなっちゃって、それがいやでたまらないんだ。

* chill「頭を冷やす；気を落ち着ける」 the center of attention「注目の的」
  kill「参らせる；圧倒する」

Stage 3　英文トランスクリプション

ドラマのシーン全体を英文の原稿で確認しながらCDで耳慣らししよう！ その上で、ドラマ・シーンの音声を聴きながら、まだできていない部分の穴埋めに再チャレンジしよう。

● ● ● ● ● ●

A Hey, ① **who was** that girl ② **that just** walked by? I haven't seen her before. Did she just transfer here?

B Oh, yeah. Natalie. I suppose you think she's super hot, right? Like every other guy?

A Well, yeah, she is ③ **pretty** hot. ④ **Is she** like a model or ⑤ **something**?

B Yeah, but she's gross. Those boobs are ⑥ **totally** fake. I think she had ⑦ **like a** nose job or something too.

A ⑧ **That just** sounds like a bunch of gossip! How do you know she ⑨ **had a** boob job?

B It's so, like, obvious! Anyway, half the guys have already ⑩ **hit on her**, so you'll have to ⑪ **get in** line, loverboy.

A Who said anything about hitting ⑫ **on her**? I just asked ⑬ **about her**.

B I saw the way you checked her out, though. You're such a douche sometimes, Vinnie.

A Better cool the jealousy, Sam. That shade of green clashes with your mascara.

B Oh, shut up. Why should I be jealous? If you ⑭ **want to** be shot down by Miss Fakey Boobs, be my guest.

A Wow, somebody needs to seriously chill. ⑮ **Little** Sammy's no longer the center of attention, and it's killing her.

Stage 4 音声変化をチェック

まとめとして、穴埋め部分の音声変化の特徴を**スロー・スピード**と**ナチュラル・スピード**で確認しよう。下記に示したカタカナ表記で音声変化を確認して、もう一度ドラマを聴き直してみよう。発音変化のルールは適宜復習しよう。

❶ who was ／ フー・ワズ ▶ フーゥズ
☞ was は弱化して [wz] と発音されることがある。

❷ that just ／ ザット・ジャスト ▶ ザッ_ジャス_
☞ 2語の末尾それぞれで、破裂音 [t] が脱落する。

❸ pretty ／ プリティー ▶ プリディ [リ] ー
☞ 破裂音 [t] が弾音化する。

❹ Is she ／ イズ・シー ▶ イッ_シー
☞ [z] + [ʃ] は類似子音の連続。[z] が脱落する。

❺ something ／ サムスィング ▶ サムスィン_
☞ 末尾の破裂音 [g] が脱落する。

❻ totally ／ トウトゥリー ▶ トウドゥ [ル] リー
☞ 中程の破裂音 [t] が弾音化する。

❼ like a ／ ライク・ア ▶ ライカ
☞ 2語が連結する。

❽ That just ／ ザット・ジャスト ▶ ザッ_ジャス_
☞ ❷ と同様の変化が生じる。

❾ had a ／ ハッド・ア ▶ ハッダ [ラ]
☞ 2語が連結する。

❿ hit on her ／ ヒット・オン・ハー ▶ ヒッド [ロ] ナー
☞ her は弱化して [ァー] と発音。3語が連結する。hit on の連結部では、破裂音 [t] が弾音化する。

⓫ get in ／ ゲット・イン ▶ ゲッディ [リ] ン
☞ 連結部で [t] 音が弾音化する。

⓬ on her ／ オン・ハー ▶ オナー
☞ on に弱化した her [ァー] が連結する。

⓭ about her ／ アバウト・ハー ▶ アバウダ [ラ] ー
☞ about に弱化した her [ァー] が連結する。連結部で [t] 音が弾音化する。

⓮ want to ／ ワント・トゥー ▶ ワナ
☞ want の破裂音 [t] が脱落しつつ、弱化した to [ァ] に連結する。

⓯ Little ／ リトゥゥ ▶ リドゥ [ル] ゥ
☞ 破裂音 [t] が弾音化する。

高校生ドラマ 93

Unit 15 ファミリー・コメディー
Family Comedy (Full House type)

Stage 1 穴埋めドラマ・リスニング

CD 1-44 CD 1-45

音声変化に注意してCDでドラマの音声を聴きながら空欄部分を埋めてみよう。CDのナチュラル音声での聴き取りが難しいときは、次のトラックに収録されたスロー音声で聴いてみよう。

● ● ● ● ●

A Dad, I ① _____ my own room.

B Sure, Allison. And where do you ② _____ _____ building it? Maybe the roof?

A Dad, I'm serious! I'm thirteen! I need my privacy!

B Honey, you know as well as I do ③ _____ we just don't have the space. You and Megan have the biggest room ④ _____ _____ whole house. You'll just have to make do.

A But Megan is ⑤ _____ _____ drive me crazy! She's so ... immature.

B Your uncle Danny says the same thing ⑥ _____ _____ Ted all the time, but THEY manage to share a room.

A Well, ⑦ _____ _____ _____ office? ⑧ _____ _____ move your stuff in with Megan, and I can stay there?

B First of all, honey, my 'office' is ⑨ _____ _____ size of a closet, as you well know. You ⑩ _____ fit half of your things

94

in there. ⑪ _____ _____ all, I need that space to work.

Ⓐ ⑫ _____ Dad! All my friends have their own rooms! Living with my kid sister is seriously cramping my style!

Ⓑ A thirteen year old girl doesn't need a 'style.' Regardless, you and Megan are just ⑬ _____ _____ have to ⑭ _____ _____ with each other.

Ⓐ You mean we'll share a room until I'm ready for college? Five more years? I wanna ⑮ _____ _____!

Stage 2 ドラマのシーン解説

日本語訳と、解説を参照しながら、ドラマの内容を確認しよう。そのあとで、Stage1の穴埋めに再チャレンジしてみよう。

Ⓐ Dad, I ① **want** my own room.

パパ、私、自分の部屋が欲しいの。

Ⓑ Sure, Allison. And where do you ② **plan on** building it? Maybe the roof?

いいとも、アリスン。で、それをどこに建てるつもりなのさ？ 屋根かなぁ？

Ⓐ Dad, I'm serious! I'm thirteen! I need my privacy!

パパ、マジメに言ってるのよ！ 私、13歳なんだから！ プライバシーが必要なの！

ファミリー・コメディー 95

🅑 Honey, you know as well as I do ③ **that** we just don't have the space. You and Megan have the biggest room ④ **in the** whole house. You'll just have to make do.

ハニー、君は、いまうちにスペースがないってことを、パパと同じくらいよくわかってるよね。君とメーガンは家全体でいちばん大きな部屋を使ってるんだよ。なんとかしてもらわないとさ。

* make do「間に合わす；済ます；折り合いをつける」

🅐 But Megan is ⑤ **starting to** drive me crazy! She's so ... immature.

でも、メーガンのことがムカついてきてるの！ すっごく、その…子どもなのよ。

* drive someone crazy「…をムカつかせる」 immature「未成熟の」

🅑 Your uncle Danny says the same thing ⑥ **about uncle** Ted all the time, but THEY manage to share a room.

君のおじさんのダニーは、テッドおじさんのことで、いつも同じことを言ってるけど、あのふたりでさえなんとか部屋をいっしょに使ってるんだ。

* manage to ...「なんとかして…する」

🅐 Well, ⑦ **what about your** office? ⑧ **Can't you** move your stuff in with Megan, and I can stay there?

あー、パパのオフィスはどうなの？ メーガンのところにパパの荷物を運べば、私がそこに入れるわよね？

* stuff「持ち物」

🅑 First of all, honey, my 'office' is ⑨ **about the** size of a closet, as you well know. You ⑩ **couldn't** fit half of your things in there. ⑪ **Second of** all, I need that space to work.

ハニー、まず第一に、よくご存じのとおり、パパのオフィスは、ほぼ押し入れサイズなんだ

よ。あそこには君の荷物の半分も入りやしないだろうさ。第二にはだよ、パパはあのスペースが仕事に必要なんだ。

Ⓐ ⑫ **But** Dad! All my friends have their own rooms! Living with my kid sister is seriously cramping my style!

でも、パパ！ 友達はみんな自分の部屋をもってるの！ 妹といっしょに暮らしてることが、私のスタイルを大幅に阻害しているのよ。

* kid sister「妹」　cramp「阻害する」

Ⓑ A thirteen year old girl doesn't need a 'style.' Regardless, you and Megan are just ⑬ **going to** have to ⑭ **put up** with each other.

13歳の女の子に「スタイル」なんて必要ないよ。いずれにしても、君とメーガンはお互いに我慢してもらうしかないね。

* Regardless, ...「いずれにせよ…」　put up with ...「…を我慢する」

Ⓐ You mean we'll share a room until I'm ready for college? Five more years? I wanna ⑮ **run away**!

私が大学に入れるまで部屋をシェアするってこと？ あと5年も？ もう家出したいわ！

* run away「逃げ出す」

Stage 3 英文トランスクリプション

ドラマのシーン全体を英文の原稿で確認しながらCDで耳慣らししよう！ その上で、ドラマ・シーンの音声を聴きながら、まだできていない部分の穴埋めに再チャレンジしよう。

• • • • •

A Dad, I ① **want** my own room.

B Sure, Allison. And where do you ② **plan on** building it? Maybe the roof?

A Dad, I'm serious! I'm thirteen! I need my privacy!

B Honey, you know as well as I do ③ **that** we just don't have the space. You and Megan have the biggest room ④ **in the** whole house. You'll just have to make do.

A But Megan is ⑤ **starting to** drive me crazy! She's so … immature.

B Your uncle Danny says the same thing ⑥ **about uncle** Ted all the time, but THEY manage to share a room.

A Well, ⑦ **what about your** office? ⑧ **Can't you** move your stuff in with Megan, and I can stay there?

B First of all, honey, my 'office' is ⑨ **about the** size of a closet, as you well know. You ⑩ **couldn't** fit half of your things in there. ⑪ **Second of** all, I need that space to work.

A ⑫ **But** Dad! All my friends have their own rooms! Living with my kid sister is seriously cramping my style!

B A thirteen year old girl doesn't need a 'style.' Regardless, you and Megan are just ⑬ **going to** have to ⑭ **put up** with each other.

A You mean we'll share a room until I'm ready for college? Five more years? I wanna ⑮ **run away**!

Stage 4 音声変化をチェック

まとめとして、穴埋め部分の音声変化の特徴を**スロー・スピード**と**ナチュラル・スピード**で確認しよう。下記に示したカタカナ表記で音声変化を確認して、もう一度ドラマを聴き直してみよう。発音変化のルールは適宜復習しよう。

❶ want ワント ▶ ワン＿
☞ 末尾の破裂音 [t] が脱落する。

❷ plan on プラン・オン ▶ プラノン
☞ 2語が連結する。

❸ that ザット ▶ ザッ＿
☞ 末尾の破裂音 [t] が脱落する。

❹ in the イン・ザ ▶ イナ
☞ [n] + [ð] が [n] 音に変化する。

❺ starting to スターティング・トゥー ▶ スターディ [リ] ン＿ドゥ [ル] ー
☞ starting の破裂音 [t] が弾音化、末尾の [g] 音が脱落する。to の [t] 音も弾音化することがある。

❻ about uncle アバウト・アンクゥ ▶ アバウダ [ラ] ンクゥ
☞ 連結部で [t] 音が弾音化する。

❼ what about your ワット・アバウト・ユァ ▶ ワッダバ [ラ] ウチュア
☞ what about の連結部で [t] 音が弾音化する。about your では、[t] + [j] の部分で音が混じり合い、[チュ] に近い音に変化する。

❽ Can't you キャント・ユー ▶ キャンチュー
☞ [t] + [j] の部分で音が混じり合い、[チュ] に近い音に変化する。

❾ about the アバウト・ザ ▶ アバウッ＿ザ
☞ about 末尾の破裂音 [t] が脱落する。

❿ couldn't クドゥント ▶ クンン＿
☞ [dn] の [d] 音が声門閉鎖音化する。末尾の [t] 音は脱落。

⓫ Second of セカンド・アヴ ▶ セカナ (ヴ)
☞ Second 末尾の [d] 音が脱落しつつ、2語が連結する。

⓬ But バット ▶ バッ＿
☞ 末尾の [t] 音が脱落する。

⓭ going to ゴウイング・トゥー ▶ ゴウイン＿トゥー
☞ going 末尾の破裂音 [g] が脱落する。

⓮ put up プット・アップ ▶ プッダ [ラ] ップ
☞ 連結部で破裂音 [t] が弾音化する。

⓯ run away ラン・アウェイ ▶ ラナウェイ
☞ 2語が連結する。

ファミリー・コメディー 99

Unit 16 歴史ドラマ
Ancient Times Drama (Game of Thrones type)

Stage 1 穴埋めドラマ・リスニング

音声変化に注意してCDでドラマの音声を聴きながら空欄部分を埋めてみよう。CDのナチュラル音声での聴き取りが難しいときは、次のトラックに収録されたスロー音声で聴いてみよう。

● ● ● ● ●

A Is my lord unable to sleep?

B Sleep? How easy can one sleep ① _____ _____ target on one's forehead?

A ② _____ _____ _____ mean? Are you in danger? Are we?

B My own sister is ③ _____ against us. She wishes to place her bastard son upon the throne.

A Catherine? But have you not told me there is no one in the kingdom you trust more than her?

B My trust was naive, ④ _____ sentimental. And badly misplaced. I'll not make that mistake again.

A It is ⑤ _____ _____ believe! When ⑥ _____ _____ become aware of her ⑦ _____?

B Just this morn, from a source I ⑧ _____. She is with some of the Northern clans. They are amassing ⑨ _____ _____

⑩ _____ _____ north shore of Tensing River.

A The witch! Does she know you are aware of her treachery?

B No, ⑪ _____ _____ soon will. At midnight my guard will lay siege to her castle. She'll be burned ⑫ _____ _____ stake if she ⑬ _____ to return.

A May the gods abandon her!

B She will pay. She has thrown in her lot with the northern clans, so she'll have to ⑭ _____ _____ _____ as ⑮ _____ _____ them.

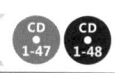

Stage 2 ドラマのシーン解説

日本語訳と、解説を参照しながら、ドラマの内容を確認しよう。そのあとで、Stage1の穴埋めに再チャレンジしてみよう。

A Is my lord unable to sleep?

わが王よ、お眠りになれませんか？

B Sleep? How easy can one sleep ① **with a** target on one's forehead?

眠る？ 額に的をつけられてどれほど気楽に寝られようか？

＊ easy「気楽な；くつろいで」 target「的；標的」

A ② **What do you** mean? Are you in danger? Are we?

どういうことでしょう？ 王は危機に瀕していらっしゃるのですか？ われわれが？

歴史ドラマ 101

* in danger「危機に陥って」

B My own sister is ③ **plotting** against us. She wishes to place her bastard son upon the throne.

私の姉が陰謀を巡らせているのだ。姉は、浮気でつくった息子を王位に就けたいのだ。

* plot against ...「…に陰謀を企む」 place A upon B「A を B (の位) に就ける」
  bastard「非嫡出の」 throne「玉座；王位；王権」

A Catherine? But have you not told me there is no one in the kingdom you trust more than her?

キャサリンがですか？ しかし、王国において彼女ほど信頼できる人物はいないと、おっしゃいませんでしたか？

* kingdom「王国」

B My trust was naive, ④ **and** sentimental. And badly misplaced. I'll not make that mistake again.

世間知らずで感傷的な信頼だったのだ。そして、ひどく見当違いだった。私は、二度と同じ間違いは繰り返さない。

* naive「単純な；素朴な；世間知らずの」 sentimental「感傷的な」 misplaced「見当違いの」

A It is ⑤ **hard to** believe! When ⑥ **did you** become aware of her ⑦ **plotting**?

それは信じがたいことです！ いつ、彼女の陰謀にお気づきに？

* become aware of ...「…に気づく」

B Just this morn, from a source I ⑧ **trust**. She is with some of the Northern clans. They are amassing ⑨ **an army** ⑩ **on the** north shore of Tensing River.

ほんの今朝だ、信頼できる筋から。姉は、北方氏族のいくつかと結託しているのだ。彼らは、テンジング河の北岸に軍隊を結集させている。

* source「情報源」 clan「氏族；一族」 amass「集める；蓄積する；集結する」

A The witch! Does she know you are aware of her treachery?

汚らしい魔女め！ あなたが裏切りに気づいていることを、知っているのでしょうか？

* witch「魔女；醜い女；いやな女」 treachery「裏切り；背信」

B No, ⑪ **but she** soon will. At midnight my guard will lay siege to her castle. She'll be burned ⑫ **at the** stake if she ⑬ **tries** to return.

いや、だが、すぐに気づくだろう。真夜中の12時に、私の兵が姉の城を包囲攻撃する。（城に）戻ろうとすれば、火あぶりの刑に処せられることになる。

* at midnight「深夜0時に」 guard「兵」 lay siege to ...「…を包囲・攻撃する」
  be burned at the stake「火あぶりの刑に処せられる」

A May the gods abandon her!

神よ、彼女を見放し給え！

* May the gods ...「神々よ…し給え」 abandon「見捨てる；見放す」

B She will pay. She has thrown in her lot with the northern clans, so she'll have to ⑭ **fight and die** as ⑮ **one of** them.

姉は報いを受けるだろう。彼女は北の氏族どもと運命を共にしたのだ。奴らの仲間として戦い、そして果てねばならない。

* pay「報いを受ける」 throw in one's lot with ...「…と運命を共にする」

歴史ドラマ 103

Stage 3 英文トランスクリプション

ドラマのシーン全体を英文の原稿で確認しながらCDで耳慣らししよう！ その上で、ドラマ・シーンの音声を聴きながら、まだできていない部分の穴埋めに再チャレンジしよう。

● ● ● ● ●

A Is my lord unable to sleep?

B Sleep? How easy can one sleep ① **with a** target on one's forehead?

A ② **What do you** mean? Are you in danger? Are we?

B My own sister is ③ **plotting** against us. She wishes to place her bastard son upon the throne.

A Catherine? But have you not told me there is no one in the kingdom you trust more than her?

B My trust was naive, ④ **and** sentimental. And badly misplaced. I'll not make that mistake again.

A It is ⑤ **hard to** believe! When ⑥ **did you** become aware of her ⑦ **plotting**?

B Just this morn, from a source I ⑧ **trust**. She is with some of the Northern clans. They are amassing ⑨ **an army** ⑩ **on the** north shore of Tensing River.

A The witch! Does she know you are aware of her treachery?

B No, ⑪ **but she** soon will. At midnight my guard will lay siege to her castle. She'll be burned ⑫ **at the** stake if she ⑬ **tries** to return.

A May the gods abandon her!

B She will pay. She has thrown in her lot with the northern clans, so she'll have to ⑭ **fight and die** as ⑮ **one of** them.

Stage 4 音声変化をチェック

まとめとして、穴埋め部分の音声変化の特徴を**スロー・スピード**と**ナチュラル・スピード**で確認しよう。下記に示したカタカナ表記で音声変化を確認して、もう一度ドラマを聴き直してみよう。発音変化のルールは適宜復習しよう。

❶ **with a**   ウィズ・ア   ▶ ウィザ
☞ 2語が連結する。

❷ **What do you**   ワット・ドゥー・ユー   ▶ ワッ＿ドゥユ
☞ What の破裂音 [t] が脱落する。do you は弱化して [ドゥユ] と短く発音される。

❸ **plotting**   プロッティング   ▶ プロッディ[リ]ン(グ)
☞ 破裂音 [t] が弾音化する。末尾の [g] 音が脱落することもある。

❹ **and**   アンド   ▶ アン＿
☞ 末尾の破裂音 [d] が脱落する。

❺ **hard to**   ハード・トゥー   ▶ ハー＿ドゥ[ル]ー
☞ hard 末尾の破裂音 [d] が脱落。to の [t] 音が弾音化する。

❻ **did you**   ディッド・ユー   ▶ ディッジュー
☞ [d] + [j] の部分で音が混じり合い、[ジュ] に近い音に変化する。

❼ **plotting**   プロッティング   ▶ プロッディ[リ]ン(グ)
☞ ❸と同様の変化が生じる。

❽ **trust**   トゥラスト   ▶ チュラスト
☞ [tr] 部分の [t] 音が [チュ] に近い音に変化する。

❾ **an army**   アン・アーミー   ▶ アナーミー
☞ 2語が連結する。

❿ **on the**   オン・ザ   ▶ オナ
☞ [n] + [ð] が [n] 音に変化する。

⓫ **but she**   バット・シー   ▶ バッ＿シー
☞ 破裂音 [t] が脱落する。

⓬ **at the**   アット・ザ   ▶ アッ＿ザ
☞ at 末尾の破裂音 [t] が脱落する。

⓭ **tries**   トゥライズ   ▶ チュライズ
☞ [tr] 部分の [t] 音が [チュ] に近い音に変化する。

⓮ **fight and die**   ファイト・アンド・ダイ   ▶ ファイタン＿ダイ
☞ fight and は連結。and 末尾の破裂音 [d] が脱落する。

⓯ **one of**   ワン・アヴ   ▶ ワナ(ヴ)
☞ 2語が連結する。末尾の [v] 音が脱落する場合もある。

Unit 17 探偵ドラマ
Detective Drama (Sherlock type)

Stage 1 穴埋めドラマ・リスニング

音声変化に注意してCDでドラマの音声を聴きながら空欄部分を埋めてみよう。CDのナチュラル音声での聴き取りが難しいときは、次のトラックに収録されたスロー音声で聴いてみよう。

● ● ● ● ●

A And how was the murder carried out?

B I am quite sure ① _____ _____ poison was slowly administered to the victim. Perhaps via wine.

A So, do you think the cook was involved in the plot?

B I have spoken ② _____ her, and I have no reason to suspect she was aware of the role she played.

A ③ _____ _____ _____ few flaws is your weakness toward the fairer sex. How can you be sure she was unaware ④ _____ _____ foul play ⑤ _____ _____?

B Such nonsense! First, of course I am NOT 'sure' ⑥ _____ _____, so far. ⑦ _____, the cook is older than my own mother and as ⑧ _____ _____ my eyes as a Jersey hog.

A But how ⑨ _____ _____ wine have been poisoned ⑩ _____ _____ knowledge of the very person who poured it?

106

B My theory is that the wine was poisoned before the cook would have ⑪ _____ _____ chance to ⑫ _____ _____ .

A But how ⑬ _____ _____ _____ accomplished? How does one poison a corked ⑭ _____ of wine?

B This is ⑮ _____ _____ have now determined to investigate. From the butler I have received a full list of every wine seller from whom Lord Dussord made his purchases.

Stage 2 ドラマのシーン解説

日本語訳と、解説を参照しながら、ドラマの内容を確認しよう。そのあとで、Stage1の穴埋めに再チャレンジしてみよう。

A And how was the murder carried out?

で、殺害はどのように行われたんだろう?

* murder「殺人」 carry out「行う；実行する」

B I am quite sure ① **that a** poison was slowly administered to the victim. Perhaps via wine.

きっと犠牲者に毒が徐々に投与されたのだろう。おそらくワインを通して。

* administer「投与する」 via ...「…を通して」

A So, do you think the cook was involved in the plot?

探偵ドラマ 107

それで、シェフが陰謀に関わっていると？

＊ involved「関わって；関与して」 plot「陰謀」

B I have spoken ② **to** her, and I have no reason to suspect she was aware of the role she played.

彼女と話をしたが、自分が果たした役割を彼女が知っていると疑う理由は見つからない。

＊ suspect「疑う；嫌疑をかける」

A ③ **One of your** few flaws is your weakness toward the fairer sex. How can you be sure she was unaware ④ **of the** foul play ⑤ **going on**?

あなたに欠点は少ないが、女性に弱いところがそのひとつだ。殺人が行われていることに彼女が気づいていなかったと、どうして確信がもてるんだい？

＊ flaw「欠点」 fair(er) sex「女性」 foul play「殺人；暴行；不正行為」

B Such nonsense! First, of course I am NOT 'sure' ⑥ **about anything**, so far. ⑦ **Secondly**, the cook is older than my own mother and as ⑧ **appealing to** my eyes as a Jersey hog.

バカげたことを！ まず、もちろん私にはなにも確信はない、これまでのところはね。次に、シェフは私の母よりも年上なのだ。それに、私の目にはジャージーのブタと同程度のアピールしかないのだ。

＊ nonsense「バカげた考え・話」 Jersey hog「(英国) ジャージー島原産のブタ」

A But how ⑨ **could the** wine have been poisoned ⑩ **without the** knowledge of the very person who poured it?

しかし、注いだ当の本人が知ることなく、どうやってワインに毒が盛られたというのだ？

＊ poison「毒する」 knowledge「認識」

Ⓑ My theory is that the wine was poisoned before the cook would have ⑪ **had a** chance to ⑫ **open it**.

私の仮説では、ワインは、シェフが空ける前に毒を盛られていたのだ。

* have a chance to ...「…する機会を得る」

Ⓐ But how ⑬ **could that be** accomplished? How does one poison a corked ⑭ **bottle** of wine?

しかし、どうやってそんなことを成すことが？　どうやってコルクの嵌まったワインに毒を盛るというのだ？

* accomplish「達成する；成就する」　corked「コルク栓をした」

Ⓑ This is ⑮ **what I** have now determined to investigate. From the butler I have received a full list of every wine seller from whom Lord Dussord made his purchases.

私はいま、これを調査しようと決めたのだ。私は執事からすべてのワイン業者のリストを受け取っている。ダソード卿がワインを購入した業者のね。

* butler「執事」　make one's purshase「購入する」

Stage 3 英文トランスクリプション

ドラマのシーン全体を英文の原稿で確認しながらCDで耳慣らししよう！ その上で、ドラマ・シーンの音声を聴きながら、まだできていない部分の穴埋めに再チャレンジしよう。

• • • • • •

A And how was the murder carried out?

B I am quite sure ① **that a** poison was slowly administered to the victim. Perhaps via wine.

A So, do you think the cook was involved in the plot?

B I have spoken ② **to** her, and I have no reason to suspect she was aware of the role she played.

A ③ **One of your** few flaws is your weakness toward the fairer sex. How can you be sure she was unaware ④ **of the** foul play ⑤ **going on**?

B Such nonsense! First, of course I am NOT 'sure' ⑥ **about anything**, so far. ⑦ **Secondly**, the cook is older than my own mother and as ⑧ **appealing to** my eyes as a Jersey hog.

A But how ⑨ **could the** wine have been poisoned ⑩ **without the** knowledge of the very person who poured it?

B My theory is that the wine was poisoned before the cook would have ⑪ **had a** chance to ⑫ **open it**.

A But how ⑬ **could that be** accomplished? How does one poison a corked ⑭ **bottle** of wine?

B This is ⑮ **what I** have now determined to investigate. From the butler I have received a full list of every wine seller from whom Lord Dussord made his purchases.

Stage 4 音声変化をチェック

まとめとして、穴埋め部分の音声変化の特徴を**スロー・スピード**と**ナチュラル・スピード**で確認しよう。下記に示したカタカナ表記で音声変化を確認して、もう一度ドラマを聴き直してみよう。発音変化のルールは適宜復習しよう。

❶ that a   ザット・ア   ▶ ザッダ [ラ]
☞ 2 語が連結。連結部で破裂音 [t] が弾音化する。

❷ to   トゥー   ▶ ドゥ [ル]
☞ to は弱化。破裂音 [t] が弾音化する。

❸ One of your   ワン・アヴ・ユア   ▶ ワナ (ヴ) ユア
☞ One of が連結。of 末尾の [v] 音が脱落することもある。

❹ of the   アヴ・ザ   ▶ アッ_ザ
☞ of 末尾の [v] 音が脱落する。

❺ going on   ゴウイング・オン   ▶ ゴウイノン
☞ going 末尾の破裂音 [g] が脱落しつつ、on に連結する。

❻ about anything   アバウト・エニスィング   ▶ アバウデ [レ] ニスィン_
☞ 2 語が連結。連結部で [t] 音が弾音化する。anything 末尾の [g] 音が脱落。

❼ Secondly   セカンドゥリー   ▶ セカン_リー
☞ [dl] で [d] 音の脱落が生じる。

❽ appealing to   アピーリング・トゥー   ▶ アピーリン_ドゥ [ル] ー
☞ appealing 末尾の [g] 音が脱落する。to は弱化し、[t] 音の弾音化も生じる。

❾ could the   クッド・ザ   ▶ クッ_ザ
☞ could 末尾の [d] 音が脱落する。

❿ without the   ウィザウト・ザ   ▶ ウィザウッ_ザ
☞ without 末尾の [t] 音が脱落する。

⓫ had a   ハッド・ア   ▶ ハッダ [ラ]
☞ 連結部で破裂音 [d] が弾音化する。

⓬ open it   オウプン・イット   ▶ オウプニット
☞ 2 語が連結する。

⓭ could that be   クッド・ザット・ビー   ▶ クッ_ザッ_ビ
☞ could や that の末尾で破裂音が脱落する。be は弱化。

⓮ bottle   バトゥゥ   ▶ バドゥ [ル] ゥ
☞ 破裂音 [t] が弾音化する。

⓯ what I   ワット・アイ   ▶ ワッダ [ラ] イ
☞ 連結部で破裂音 [t] が弾音化する。

Unit 18 ゾンビ・ドラマ
Zombie Drama (Walking Dead type)

Stage 1 穴埋めドラマ・リスニング

音声変化に注意してCDでドラマの音声を聴きながら空欄部分を埋めてみよう。CDのナチュラル音声での聴き取りが難しいときは、次のトラックに収録されたスロー音声で聴いてみよう。

● ● ● ● ●

A We've got the windows and doors boarded up. And people standing watch.

B Okay, that's good. ① _____ we're gonna need ammo, and ② _____ _____ food. There's a gun shop and a ③ _____ grocery ④ _____ _____ mile up the road.

A That ⑤ _____ _____ us much good. The zombies are ⑥ _____ _____ this house!

B Soon as we put the fire out, I'll ⑦ _____ _____ run up the chimney and over to my van.

A That's a suicide mission. They can smell your blood. You won't ⑧ _____ _____ ⑨ _____ yards before …

B Well, ⑩ _____ _____ options do we have? If we just stay put, they'll ⑪ _____ _____ out.

A Before you do that, let's make a thorough search of this place. Maybe we can find something to use against them.

112

B Okay. As unlikely as ⑫ _____ _____ ⑬ _____ we'll find something, we might get lucky. If not, we'll go with my plan. Agreed?

A Okay. Let's search the ⑭ _____. Maybe we can find some kerosene or something we can use to burn them.

B Listen! Do you hear that?

A What, what?

B They're ⑮ _____ _____ come through the chimney! Quick! Get your gun up there and start blasting!

Stage 2 ドラマのシーン解説

日本語訳と、解説を参照しながら、ドラマの内容を確認しよう。そのあとで、Stage1の穴埋めに再チャレンジしてみよう。

A We've got the windows and doors boarded up. And people standing watch.

窓とドアは板で塞いだ。そして、見張りを立たせている。

* board up「板で塞ぐ」 stand watch「警備につく」2語でひとつの動詞。

B Okay, that's good. ① **But** we're gonna need ammo, and ② **some more** food. There's a gun shop and a ③ **little** grocery ④ **about a** mile up the road.

わかった。いいだろう。しかし、弾薬、それに食糧の追加が必要だ。1マイルほど行ったところに、銃器店と小さな食料品店がある。

＊ ammo = ammunition「弾薬」

A That ⑤ **doesn't do** us much good. The zombies are ⑥ **right outside** this house!

それは、あまり得策じゃない。ゾンビはこの家のすぐ外にいるんだぞ！

＊ do ... good「…の役に立つ；得になる」

B Soon as we put the fire out, I'll ⑦ **make a** run up the chimney and over to my van.

火を消したらすぐに、俺は急いで煙突を登って外に出て、バンまで走る。

＊ chimney「煙突」

A That's a suicide mission. They can smell your blood. You won't ⑧ **make it** ⑨ **twenty** yards before ...

それは自殺的なミッションだよ。奴らは、君の血を嗅ぎ分けられる。20ヤード進まないうちに、君は…

＊ mission「任務」

B Well, ⑩ **what other** options do we have? If we just stay put, they'll ⑪ **wait us** out.

じゃあ、俺たちに残されたほかの選択肢は？ 俺たちがじっとしていれば、奴らは僕らが根負けするまで待ち続けるよ。

＊ option「選択肢」　stay put「動かないでいる；じっとしている」
　wait ... out「根負けさせるまで…を待つ」

A Before you do that, let's make a thorough search of this place. Maybe we can find something to use against them.

114

君がそうする前に、この場所を徹底的に調べよう。おそらく奴らに立ち向かうために使える なにかを発見できるかもしれない。

* thorough「徹底的な」

B Okay. As unlikely as ⑫ **it is** ⑬ **that** we'll find something, we might get lucky. If not, we'll go with my plan. Agreed?

わかった。なにかを見つけられそうにはないが、運よく運ぶかもしれない。もしダメなら、俺のプランでいく。いいな？

* unlikely「ありそうもない」 get lucky「運よく成功する」

A Okay. Let's search the ⑭ **attic**. Maybe we can find some kerosene or something we can use to burn them.

わかったよ。屋根裏を探してみよう。奴らを燃やせる灯油かなにかを見つけられるかも。

* attic「屋根裏」 kerosene「灯油」 burn「燃やす」

B Listen! Do you hear that?

しっ！ あれが聞こえるか？

A What, what?

えっ、なんだ？

B They're ⑮ **trying to** come through the chimney! Quick! Get your gun up there and start blasting!

奴ら、煙突から入ってこようとしてる！ 急げ！ 拳銃を上に向けて撃ちまくるんだ！

* blast「連射する；撃つ；射殺する」

Stage 3 英文トランスクリプション

ドラマのシーン全体を英文の原稿で確認しながらCDで耳慣らししよう！ その上で、ドラマ・シーンの音声を聴きながら、まだできていない部分の穴埋めに再チャレンジしよう。

● ● ● ● ● ●

A We've got the windows and doors boarded up. And people standing watch.

B Okay, that's good. ① **But** we're gonna need ammo, and ② **some more** food. There's a gun shop and a ③ **little** grocery ④ **about a** mile up the road.

A That ⑤ **doesn't do** us much good. The zombies are ⑥ **right outside** this house!

B Soon as we put the fire out, I'll ⑦ **make a** run up the chimney and over to my van.

A That's a suicide mission. They can smell your blood. You won't ⑧ **make it** ⑨ **twenty** yards before …

B Well, ⑩ **what other** options do we have? If we just stay put, they'll ⑪ **wait us** out.

A Before you do that, let's make a thorough search of this place. Maybe we can find something to use against them.

B Okay. As unlikely as ⑫ **it is** ⑬ **that** we'll find something, we might get lucky. If not, we'll go with my plan. Agreed?

A Okay. Let's search the ⑭ **attic**. Maybe we can find some kerosene or something we can use to burn them.

B Listen! Do you hear that?

A What, what?

B They're ⑮ **trying to** come through the chimney! Quick! Get your gun up there and start blasting!

Stage 4 音声変化をチェック

まとめとして、穴埋め部分の音声変化の特徴を**スロー・スピード**と**ナチュラル・スピード**で確認しよう。下記に示したカタカナ表記で音声変化を確認して、もう一度ドラマを聴き直してみよう。発音変化のルールは適宜復習しよう。

❶ But バット ▶ バッ＿
☞ 末尾の破裂音 [t] が脱落する。

❷ some more サム・モー ▶ サ＿モー
☞ 子音 [m] の連続で片方が脱落する。

❸ little リトゥゥ ▶ リドゥ [ル] ゥ
☞ 破裂音 [t] が弾音化する。

❹ about a ァバウト・ア ▶ ァバウダ [ラ]
☞ 連結部で [t] 音が弾音化する。

❺ doesn't do ダズント・ドゥー ▶ ダズン＿ドゥー
☞ doesn't 末尾の破裂音 [t] が脱落する。

❻ right outside ライト・アウトサイド ▶ ライダ [ラ] ウッ＿サイ (ド)
☞ 2語が連結。連結部で [t] 音が弾音化する。outside 中程の [t] 音、末尾の [d] 音が脱落する場合がある。

❼ make a メイク・ア ▶ メイカ
☞ 2語が連結する。

❽ make it メイク・イット ▶ メイキッ＿
☞ 2語が連結。it 末尾の [t] 音が脱落する。

❾ twenty トゥエンティー ▶ トゥエニー
☞ [nt] で [t] 音の脱落が生じる。

❿ what other ワット・アザー ▶ ワッダ [ラ] ザー
☞ 2語が連結。連結部で [t] 音が弾音化する。

⓫ wait us ウェイト・アス ▶ ウェイダ [ラ] ス
☞ 連結部で [t] 音が弾音化する。

⓬ it is イット・イズ ▶ イッディ [リ] ズ
☞ 連結部で [t] 音が弾音化する。

⓭ that ザット ▶ ザッ＿
☞ 末尾の破裂音 [t] が脱落する。

⓮ attic アッティック ▶ アッディ [リ] ック
☞ 破裂音 [t] が弾音化する。

⓯ trying to トゥライイング・トゥー ▶ トゥラインヌ
☞ trying 末尾の破裂音 [g] が脱落し、弱化した to [ゥ] に連結。

ゾンビ・ドラマ 117

Unit 19 ヴァンパイア・ドラマ

Vampire Drama (Twilight type)

Stage 1 穴埋めドラマ・リスニング

音声変化に注意してCDでドラマの音声を聴きながら空欄部分を埋めてみよう。CDのナチュラル音声での聴き取りが難しいときは、次のトラックに収録されたスロー音声で聴いてみよう。

● ● ● ● ●

A Elsa, I've planned a ① _____ game I think you ② _____ _____.

B A game, Herman? What ③ _____ _____ _____ game?

A I shall hold a masquerade ④ _____ here ⑤ _____ _____ palace.

B Oh, now that sounds fun! And many ⑥ _____ will be invited?

A Of course! I'll make sure that there are lots of ⑦ _____ mortals to choose from!

B Ha ha, how they love these sorts of balls, don't they? They dress up as ghouls and demons ⑧ _____ _____ _____ ⑨ _____ themselves.

A Indeed, and for the two of us ⑩ _____ _____ be a come-as-you-are party!

B Just the two of us? You're not thinking to ⑪ _____ _____ friends?

A No, my dear. ⑫ _____ _____ _____ too risky. If a large number of guests don't make their way home to their safe warm beds, we will be exposed and ⑬ _____ _____.

B I see. And what makes you think we'll be safe if even two guests go missing?

A Darling, ⑭ _____ _____ know me by now? I've already arranged for there to be a terrible traffic accident that evening.

B Herman, you think of everything! And now I've ⑮ _____ _____ plan my costume! I want to be devilishly sexy!

Stage 2 ドラマのシーン解説

日本語訳と、解説を参照しながら、ドラマの内容を確認しよう。そのあとで、Stage1の穴埋めに再チャレンジしてみよう。

A Elsa, I've planned a ① **little** game I think you ② **might enjoy**.

エルサ、君に楽しんでもらえるかもと思ってちょっとしたゲームを計画したんだよ。

B A game, Herman? What ③ **sort of a** game?

ハーマン、ゲームって？ どんなゲームなの？

A I shall hold a masquerade ④ **party** here ⑤ **at the** palace.

この宮殿で仮装パーティーを開催するのさ。

* masquerade party「仮装パーティー」 palace「宮殿；豪華な建物」

ヴァンパイア・ドラマ 119

B Oh, now that sounds fun! And many ⑥ **mortals** will be invited?

へえ、それはおもしろそう！ で、多くの人間どもが招待されるのね？

* mortal「死ぬ運命にある者」ここでは命に限りのある存在、つまり「人間」のこと。

A Of course! I'll make sure that there are lots of ⑦ **beautiful** mortals to choose from!

もちろんさ！ 必ず、たくさんの美しい人間が来て、そいつらから選べるようにするからね！

* make sure that ...「…を確保する」

B Ha ha, how they love these sorts of balls, don't they? They dress up as ghouls and demons ⑧ **and try to** ⑨ **frighten** themselves.

ハハ、あいつらは、こういった舞踏会がものすごく好きよね？ グールやディーモンの格好に着飾って互いを脅かそうとするのよ。

* ball「舞踏会 ; ダンス・パーティー」

A Indeed, and for the two of us ⑩ **it will** be a come-as-you-are party!

そうさ、それに僕らふたりにとっては、普段着のパーティーってことになる！

* come as you are「普段着でお越しください」

B Just the two of us? You're not thinking to ⑪ **invite our** friends?

私たちふたりだけなの？ 友達を招待することは考えてないの？

A No, my dear. ⑫ **That would be** too risky. If a large number of guests don't make their way home to their safe warm beds, we will be exposed and ⑬ **hunted down**.

考えてないよ、僕のかわいい人。それはリスクが大きすぎる。多くのゲストが彼らの家の暖

かくて安全なベッドに戻れなきゃ、僕らは正体を暴かれ、捕殺されてしまうだろう。

* dear「かわいい人;愛しい人」 expose「正体を暴く」 hunt down「追跡して捕まえる;追跡して殺す」

B I see. And what makes you think we'll be safe if even two guests go missing?

そうね。それに、あなたはどうして、たとえふたりのゲストがいなくなっても、私たちが安全だって思うの？

* go missing「失踪する」

A Darling, ⑭ **don't you** know me by now? I've already arranged for there to be a terrible traffic accident that evening.

ダーリン、まだ僕のことがわかってないのかい？ その晩には、ひどい交通事故が起こるように、すでに手はずを整えてあるんだよ。

* arrange「手配する」 traffic accident「交通事故」

B Herman, you think of everything! And now I've ⑮ **got to** plan my costume! I want to be devilishly sexy!

ハーマン、あなたって天才！ じゃあ、私は衣装を考えなきゃ！ 私、悪魔的にセクシーになりたいわ！

* devilishly「悪魔的に；悪女的に」

Stage 3　英文トランスクリプション

ドラマのシーン全体を英文の原稿で確認しながらCDで耳慣らししよう！ その上で、ドラマ・シーンの音声を聴きながら、まだできていない部分の穴埋めに再チャレンジしよう。

● ● ● ● ● ●

A Elsa, I've planned a ① **little** game I think you ② **might enjoy**.

B A game, Herman? What ③ **sort of a** game?

A I shall hold a masquerade ④ **party** here ⑤ **at the** palace.

B Oh, now that sounds fun! And many ⑥ **mortals** will be invited?

A Of course! I'll make sure that there are lots of ⑦ **beautiful** mortals to choose from!

B Ha ha, how they love these sorts of balls, don't they? They dress up as ghouls and demons ⑧ **and try to** ⑨ **frighten** themselves.

A Indeed, and for the two of us ⑩ **it will** be a come-as-you-are party!

B Just the two of us? You're not thinking to ⑪ **invite our** friends?

A No, my dear. ⑫ **That would be** too risky. If a large number of guests don't make their way home to their safe warm beds, we will be exposed and ⑬ **hunted down**.

B I see. And what makes you think we'll be safe if even two guests go missing?

A Darling, ⑭ **don't you** know me by now? I've already arranged for there to be a terrible traffic accident that evening.

B Herman, you think of everything! And now I've ⑮ **got to** plan my costume! I want to be devilishly sexy!

122

Stage 4　音声変化をチェック

まとめとして、穴埋め部分の音声変化の特徴を**スロー・スピード**と**ナチュラル・スピード**で確認しよう。下記に示したカタカナ表記で音声変化を確認して、もう一度ドラマを聴き直してみよう。発音変化のルールは適宜復習しよう。

❶ little 　　　　　　　　　リトゥゥ　　　　　　▶ リドゥ [ル] ゥ
　☞ 破裂音 [t] が弾音化する。

❷ might enjoy 　　　　　　マイト・エンジョイ　　▶ マイデ [レ] ンジョイ
　☞ 連結部で [t] 音が弾音化する。

❸ sort of a 　　　　　　　ソート・アヴ・ア　　　▶ ソーダ [ラ] ヴァ
　☞ 3 語が連結する。sort of の連結部で [t] 音が弾音化する。

❹ party 　　　　　　　　　パーティー　　　　　　▶ パーディ [リ] ー
　☞ 破裂音 [t] が弾音化する。

❺ at the 　　　　　　　　　アット・ザ　　　　　　▶ アッ_ザ
　☞ at 末尾の破裂音 [t] が脱落する。

❻ mortals 　　　　　　　　モータゥズ　　　　　　▶ モーダ [ラ] ゥズ
　☞ 破裂音 [t] が弾音化する。

❼ beautiful 　　　　　　　ビューティフゥ　　　　▶ ビューディ [リ] フゥ
　☞ 破裂音 [t] が弾音化する。

❽ and try to 　　　　　　　アンド・トゥライ・トゥー　▶ アン_トゥライドゥ [ル] ー
　☞ and 末尾の [d] 音が脱落。to の破裂音 [t] が弾音化する。

❾ frighten 　　　　　　　　フライトゥン　　　　　▶ フライんン
　☞ [tn] の部分が声門閉鎖音化する。

❿ it will 　　　　　　　　　イット・ウィゥ　　　　▶ イッドゥ [ル] ゥ
　☞ it が弱化した will [əl] に連結する。連結部で it の破裂音 [t] が弾音化する。

⓫ invite our 　　　　　　　インヴァイト・アゥア　　▶ インヴァイダ [ラ] ゥア
　☞ 連結部で [t] 音が弾音化する。

⓬ That would be 　　　　　ザット・ウッド・ビー　　▶ ザッ_ウッ_ビー
　☞ That, would の両語末尾の破裂音が脱落する。

⓭ hunted down 　　　　　　ハンティッド・ダウン　　▶ ハンティッ_ダウン
　☞ hunted 末尾の破裂音 [d] が脱落する。

⓮ don't you 　　　　　　　ドウント・ユー　　　　　▶ ドンチュー
　☞ don't は弱化。2 語の連結部の [t] + [j] で音が混じり合い、[チュ] に近い音に変化する。

⓯ got to 　　　　　　　　　ガット・トゥー　　　　　▶ ガッ_トゥー
　☞ got の破裂音 [t] が脱落する。

Unit 20 ファミリー・ドラマ

Family Drama (Heartland type)

Stage 1 穴埋めドラマ・リスニング

音声変化に注意してCDでドラマの音声を聴きながら空欄部分を埋めてみよう。CDのナチュラル音声での聴き取りが難しいときは、次のトラックに収録されたスロー音声で聴いてみよう。

● ● ● ● ●

A Mom, I don't really want to go to Dad's place this weekend ...

B Honey, is this about Karen? I'm ① _____ _____ two aren't ② _____ along.

A She's not really the problem. Exactly. But ③ _____ _____ changed a lot since ④ _____ remarried.

B I was kind of afraid of that, Julian. ⑤ _____ _____ like now?

A Well, for one thing, he ⑥ _____ so hard to make it like WE are a family. I'm sorry, but we're not!

B If he ⑦ _____ do that, do you think you and Karen ⑧ _____ _____ _____ okay?

A We might, ⑨ _____ _____ again we might not. I mean, to me, she's just this lady I hardly know. There's no WAY I'm ⑩ _____ _____ ⑪ _____ _____ 'mom' or anything.

B ⑫ _____ _____ father only sees you three or four times a month. He wants so much to be a ⑬ _____ _____ your life.

Ⓐ I know, ⑭ _____ _____ ⑮ _____ _____ I'm a little kid anymore either. I've got my sports; I've got my friends.

Ⓑ Have you talked at all with him about this?

Ⓐ There's no time! Every time I go over there he tries to get me to 'bond' with Karen. It's always the three of us.

Ⓑ I'll talk to him, sport. Maybe we can cut your visits down.

Stage 2 ドラマのシーン解説

日本語訳と、解説を参照しながら、ドラマの内容を確認しよう。そのあとで、Stage1の穴埋めに再チャレンジしてみよう。

Ⓐ Mom, I don't really want to go to Dad's place this weekend …

ママ、今度の週末はパパのところへあんまり行きたくないんだ…

Ⓑ Honey, is this about Karen? I'm ① **worried you** two aren't ② **getting** along.

ハニー、カレンのこと？ ママは、ふたりが仲よくやってないのが心配なのよ。

* get along「仲よくする」

Ⓐ She's not really the problem. Exactly. But ③ **Dad has** changed a lot since ④ **getting** remarried.

ファミリー・ドラマ 125

彼女がほんとうの問題じゃないんだよ。厳密にはね。でも。パパは再婚してから、ずいぶん変わっちゃったんだよ。

* get remarried「再婚する」

B I was kind of afraid of that, Julian. ⑤ **What's it** like now?

それをちょっと心配してたのよ、ジュリアン。いまは、どんなふうなの？

A Well, for one thing, he ⑥ **tries** so hard to make it like WE are a family. I'm sorry, but we're not!

うん、まずひとつには、僕らをひとつの家族みたいにしようと懸命なんだ。残念ながらそうじゃないのにさ！

* try hard「懸命に努力する」

B If he ⑦ **didn't** do that, do you think you and Karen ⑧ **would get on** okay?

パパがそうしなければ、あなたとカレンはうまくやれると思う？

* get on = get along

A We might, ⑨ **and then** again we might not. I mean, to me, she's just this lady I hardly know. There's no WAY I'm ⑩ **going to** ⑪ **call her** 'mom' or anything.

そうかも、そしてそれでもまだダメかもしれないよ。つまりね、僕にとって彼女はほぼなにも知らない女性ってだけなんだよ。彼女のことを「ママ」とかなんとか呼ぶのは、絶対に無理なんだ。

* again「また一方で」 hardly ...「ほとんど…ない」 There's no way ...「…は無理だ」

B ⑫ **But your** father only sees you three or four times a month. He wants so much to be a ⑬ **part of** your life.

でも、パパは月に 3 回か 4 回しかあなたに会えないのよ。彼は、とても強くあなたの人生の一部になりたがっているわ。

Ⓐ I know, ⑭ **but it's** ⑮ **not like** I'm a little kid anymore either. I've got my sports; I've got my friends.

わかってる。でも、僕だってもう小っちゃな子どもみたいではないんだよ。運動だってしてるし、友達だっているんだ。

* it's not like ... 「…のようではない」

Ⓑ Have you talked at all with him about this?

この件でパパとは少しでも話をしたことがあるの？

* at all 「少しでも」

Ⓐ There's no time! Every time I go over there he tries to get me to 'bond' with Karen. It's always the three of us.

時間がないんだよ！ 向こうに行くといつだって、カレンと僕を親密にしようとしてばかりなんだよ。いつだって 3 人いっしょなのさ。

* every time ... 「…するたびごとに」 bond 「絆で結ぶ；親密につなぐ」

Ⓑ I'll talk to him, sport. Maybe we can cut your visits down.

ママがパパに話してみるわよ。たぶん、あなたの訪問を減らせるでしょう。

* sport 「君」子どもなどに対するやや上から目線の呼びかけ。 cut ... down 「…を減らす；削減する」

Stage 3 英文トランスクリプション

ドラマのシーン全体を英文の原稿で確認しながらCDで耳慣らししよう！ その上で、ドラマ・シーンの音声を聴きながら、まだできていない部分の穴埋めに再チャレンジしよう。

• • • • • •

A Mom, I don't really want to go to Dad's place this weekend ...

B Honey, is this about Karen? I'm ① **worried you** two aren't ② **getting** along.

A She's not really the problem. Exactly. But ③ **Dad has** changed a lot since ④ **getting** remarried.

B I was kind of afraid of that, Julian. ⑤ **What's it** like now?

A Well, for one thing, he ⑥ **tries** so hard to make it like WE are a family. I'm sorry, but we're not!

B If he ⑦ **didn't** do that, do you think you and Karen ⑧ **would get on** okay?

A We might, ⑨ **and then** again we might not. I mean, to me, she's just this lady I hardly know. There's no WAY I'm ⑩ **going to** ⑪ **call her** 'mom' or anything.

B ⑫ **But your** father only sees you three or four times a month. He wants so much to be a ⑬ **part of** your life.

A I know, ⑭ **but it's** ⑮ **not like** I'm a little kid anymore either. I've got my sports; I've got my friends.

B Have you talked at all with him about this?

A There's no time! Every time I go over there he tries to get me to 'bond' with Karen. It's always the three of us.

B I'll talk to him, sport. Maybe we can cut your visits down.

128

Stage 4 音声変化をチェック

まとめとして、穴埋め部分の音声変化の特徴を**スロー・スピード**と**ナチュラル・スピード**で確認しよう。下記に示したカタカナ表記で音声変化を確認して、もう一度ドラマを聴き直してみよう。発音変化のルールは適宜復習しよう。

❶ **worried you** ウォーリード・ユー ▶ ウォーリージュー
☞ [d]＋[j] の部分で音が混じり合い、[ジュ] に近い音に変化する。

❷ **getting** ゲッティング ▶ ゲッディ[リ]ング
☞ 破裂音 [t] が弾音化する。

❸ **Dad has** ダッド・ハズ ▶ ダッダ[ラ]ズ
☞ Dad が弱化した has [əz] に連結。連結部で [d] 音が弾音化する。

❹ **getting** ゲッティング ▶ ゲッディ[リ]ング
☞ ❷と同様の変化が生じる。

❺ **What's it** ワッツ・イット ▶ ワッツィッ＿
☞ 2語が連結する。it 末尾の破裂音 [t] が脱落する。

❻ **tries** トゥライズ ▶ チュライズ
☞ [tr] の [t] 音は [チュ] のように変化する。

❼ **didn't** ディドゥント ▶ ディンン＿
☞ [dn] の [d] 音が声門閉鎖音化する。末尾の破裂音 [t] は脱落しやすい。

❽ **would get on** ウッド・ゲット・オン ▶ ウッ＿ゲッド[ロ]ン
☞ would 末尾の [d] 音が脱落。get on の連結部で破裂音 [t] が弾音化する。

❾ **and then** アンド・ゼン ▶ アネン
☞ and の [d] 音が脱落しながら2語が連結。[n]＋[ð] が [n] 音に変化する。

❿ **going to** ゴウイング・トゥー ▶ ゴナ
☞ 極端に変化し、[ゴナ] と発音される。

⓫ **call her** コーゥ・ハー ▶ コーラー
☞ call が弱化した her [ər] に連結。

⓬ **But your** バット・ユア ▶ バッチュア
☞ [t]＋[j] の部分で音が混じり合い、[チュ] に近い音に変化する。

⓭ **part of** パート・アヴ ▶ パーダ[ラ]ヴ
☞ 連結部で破裂音 [t] が弾音化する。

⓮ **but it's** バット・イッツ ▶ バッディ[リ]ッツ
☞ 連結部で破裂音 [t] が弾音化する。

⓯ **not like** ナット・ライク ▶ ナッ＿ライク
☞ not の破裂音 [t] が脱落する。

ファミリー・ドラマ 129

Unit 21 ゴースト・ドラマ
Ghost Drama (Supernatural type)

Stage 1 穴埋めドラマ・リスニング

音声変化に注意してCDでドラマの音声を聴きながら空欄部分を埋めてみよう。CDのナチュラル音声での聴き取りが難しいときは、次のトラックに収録されたスロー音声で聴いてみよう。

● ● ● ● ●

A So ① _____ _____ _____ that you do, exactly?

B I debunk pseudoscientific claims.

A So in other words, you're ② _____ _____ prove this house isn't haunted.

B That's ③ _____ right. And it won't be the first time I've ④ _____ _____.

A Just so I get you, you don't think there's anything ⑤ _____ _____ that ⑥ _____ _____ considered paranormal or supernatural?

B I don't see any evidence of it, whatsoever. ⑦ _____ _____ DO see evidence for is the human brain's ⑧ _____ _____ fool itself.

A So, naturally, that's ⑨ _____ _____ think my brain does. For a living.

B Well, yes. Inasmuch as you think you are here to investigate who or ⑩ _____ _____ ⑪ _____ this house that I claim ISN'T haunted, yes.

A ⑫ _____ _____ guess to you I'm a kook, huh?

B Maybe I would phrase ⑬ _____ _____ _____ ⑭ _____. And what do you think of ME as?

A As someone with a closed mind and a limited perspective. And someone who puts too much faith in science.

B Well, in a day or two perhaps we'll know which of us is correct.

A Yes. And I am guessing that will happen when you start screaming your head off ⑮ _____ _____ middle of the night.

Stage 2 ドラマのシーン解説

日本語訳と、解説を参照しながら、ドラマの内容を確認しよう。そのあとで、Stage1の穴埋めに再チャレンジしてみよう。

A So ① **what is it** that you do, exactly?

で、君がやっていることはなんなの、正確には？

B I debunk pseudoscientific claims.

非科学的な主張の間違いを証明するのよ。

＊ debunk「間違い・事実誤認を証明する；地位を低下させる」 pseudoscientific「疑似科学の」 claim「主張」

A So in other words, you're ② **here to** prove this house isn't haunted.

で、言い換えると、君はこの家が取り憑かれていないと証明するためにここに来たんだね。

B That's ③ **exactly** right. And it won't be the first time I've ④ **done that**.

まさしくそのとおりよ。それに、私はこれまでにも証明してきたの。

A Just so I get you, you don't think there's anything ⑤ **out there** that ⑥ **could be** considered paranormal or supernatural?

君の話を理解したいだけなんだけどさ、君は世の中には、科学で証明できない、あるいは超常現象だと考えられるかもしれないものはなにもないと思ってるんだね。

* Just so I get you, ... 「ただ君を理解したいだけなのだが…」 paranormal 「科学で説明のつかない」 supernatural 「超自然の」

B I don't see any evidence of it, whatsoever. ⑦ **What I** DO see evidence for is the human brain's ⑧ **ability to** fool itself.

少しもそんな証拠は見当たらないわ。私が証拠を知っているのは、自身を欺くことができる人間の脳の能力についてなの。

* evidence 「根拠；証拠」 whatsoever 「少しも」 fool 「欺く；だます」

A So, naturally, that's ⑨ **what you** think my brain does. For a living.

で、当然、君はそれを僕の脳がやっていると。職業として。

* for a living 「職業として」

B Well, yes. Inasmuch as you think you are here to investigate who or ⑩ **what is** ⑪ **haunting** this house that I claim ISN'T haunted, yes.

ええ、そうよ。取り憑かれていないと私が主張しているこの家に、だれが、あるいは、なにが取り憑いているのかを調べにここに来たとあなたが思っている限りは、そのとおりよ。

* Inasmuch as ...「…である限りは」

Ⓐ ⑫ **And I** guess to you I'm a kook, huh?

すると、僕の予想では、君にとって僕は変人ってことかい?

* kook「変人」

Ⓑ Maybe I would phrase ⑬ **it a bit** ⑭ **differently**. And what do you think of ME as?

おそらく、私ならちょっと別の表現にするわね。で、あなたは私のことをどう思っているのよ?

* phrase ...「…を言葉で表現する」

Ⓐ As someone with a closed mind and a limited perspective. And someone who puts too much faith in science.

意固地で視野の狭いだれかさんかな。それに、あまりにも科学に信頼をおいている人物だね。

* closed mind「人の説を聞き入れない閉ざされた心」
  limited perspective「狭く限られたものの見方」　put faith in ...「…に信頼をおく」

Ⓑ Well, in a day or two perhaps we'll know which of us is correct.

そうね、おそらく1日か2日で、私たちのどっちが正しいかはわかるわよ。

Ⓐ Yes. And I am guessing that will happen when you start screaming your head off ⑮ **in the** middle of the night.

ああ。それに、それが真夜中に君が絶叫し始めるときに起こると、僕は思ってるよ。

* scream one's head off「声を限りに絶叫する」

ゴースト・ドラマ　133

Stage 3 英文トランスクリプション

ドラマのシーン全体を英文の原稿で確認しながらCDで耳慣らししよう！ その上で、ドラマ・シーンの音声を聴きながら、まだできていない部分の穴埋めに再チャレンジしよう。

● ● ● ● ● ●

A So ① **what is it** that you do, exactly?

B I debunk pseudoscientific claims.

A So in other words, you're ② **here to** prove this house isn't haunted.

B That's ③ **exactly** right. And it won't be the first time I've ④ **done that**.

A Just so I get you, you don't think there's anything ⑤ **out there** that ⑥ **could be** considered paranormal or supernatural?

B I don't see any evidence of it, whatsoever. ⑦ **What I** DO see evidence for is the human brain's ⑧ **ability to** fool itself.

A So, naturally, that's ⑨ **what you** think my brain does. For a living.

B Well, yes. Inasmuch as you think you are here to investigate who or ⑩ **what is** ⑪ **haunting** this house that I claim ISN'T haunted, yes.

A ⑫ **And I** guess to you I'm a kook, huh?

B Maybe I would phrase ⑬ **it a bit** ⑭ **differently**. And what do you think of ME as?

A As someone with a closed mind and a limited perspective. And someone who puts too much faith in science.

B Well, in a day or two perhaps we'll know which of us is correct.

A Yes. And I am guessing that will happen when you start screaming your head off ⑮ **in the** middle of the night.

Stage 4 音声変化をチェック

まとめとして、穴埋め部分の音声変化の特徴を**スロー・スピード**と**ナチュラル・スピード**で確認しよう。下記に示したカタカナ表記で音声変化を確認して、もう一度ドラマを聴き直してみよう。発音変化のルールは適宜復習しよう。

❶ **what is it** 　　　　　　　　ワット・イズ・イット　　　▶ ワッディ [リ] ズィッ__
☞ 3 語が連結。what is の連結部で破裂音 [t] が弾音化する。it 末尾の [t] 音も脱落しやすい。

❷ **here to** 　　　　　　　　　ヒア・トゥー　　　　　　　▶ ヒアドゥ [ル] ー
☞ to の破裂音 [t] が弾音化する。

❸ **exactly** 　　　　　　　　　エグザクトゥリー　　　　　▶ エグザック__リー
☞ [tl] で [t] 音の脱落が生じる。

❹ **done that** 　　　　　　　　ダン・ザット　　　　　　　▶ ダナッ__
☞ 連結部の [n] + [ð] が [n] 音に変化する。that 末尾の [t] 音も脱落しやすい。

❺ **out there** 　　　　　　　　アウト・ゼア　　　　　　　▶ アウッ__ゼア
☞ out 末尾の破裂音 [t] が脱落する。

❻ **could be** 　　　　　　　　クッド・ビー　　　　　　　▶ クッ__ビー
☞ could 末尾の破裂音 [d] が脱落する。

❼ **What I** 　　　　　　　　　ワット・アイ　　　　　　　▶ ワッダ [ラ] イ
☞ 連結部で [t] 音が弾音化する。

❽ **ability to** 　　　　　　　　アビリティー・トゥー　　　▶ アビリディ [リ] ードゥ [ル] ー
☞ 2 語のそれぞれで、破裂音 [t] が弾音化する。

❾ **what you** 　　　　　　　　ワット・ユー　　　　　　　▶ ワッ__ユー
☞ what 末尾の破裂音 [t] が脱落する。

❿ **what is** 　　　　　　　　　ワット・イズ　　　　　　　▶ ワッディ [リ] ズ
☞ 連結部で [t] 音が弾音化する。

⓫ **haunting** 　　　　　　　　ホーンティング　　　　　　▶ ホーニング
☞ [nt] で [t] 音の脱落が生じる。

⓬ **And I** 　　　　　　　　　アンド・アイ　　　　　　　▶ アナイ
☞ And から [d] 音が脱落しつつ、I に連結する。

⓭ **it a bit** 　　　　　　　　　イット・ア・ビット　　　　▶ イッダ [ラ] ビッ__
☞ it a の連結部で [t] 音が弾音化する。bit 末尾の破裂音 [t] は脱落。

⓮ **differently** 　　　　　　　ディファラントゥリー　　　▶ ディファランッ__リー
☞ [tl] で [t] 音の脱落が生じる。

⓯ **in the** 　　　　　　　　　イン・ザ　　　　　　　　　▶ イナ
☞ [n] + [ð] が [n] 音に変化する。

ゴースト・ドラマ 135

Unit 22 オタク・コメディー
Geek Comedy (Big Bang Theory type)

Stage 1 穴埋めドラマ・リスニング

音声変化に注意してCDでドラマの音声を聴きながら空欄部分を埋めてみよう。CDのナチュラル音声での聴き取りが難しいときは、次のトラックに収録されたスロー音声で聴いてみよう。

● ● ● ● ●

A Todd, all this scientific mumbo jumbo you're throwing ① _____ _____ ② _____ seem to be making her heart go ③ _____ _____.

B I know! I'm ④ _____ _____! ⑤ _____ _____ don't know ⑥ _____ _____ to do!

A Maybe it's time to face facts, Einstein.

B ⑦ _____ _____ _____ those facts be?

A She's ⑧ _____ _____ you. And she's NOT into science. She only pretended to be interested in BOTH subjects to ⑨ _____ _____ _____ help her with her exams.

B You're right! You're always right. But how could she just toy with me like that? What kind of a woman ⑩ _____ _____?

A She's just a woman who is way ⑪ _____ _____ your league, that's all. She uses guys like you because she knows you'll fall for it hook, line and sinker.

B I'm sunk! I can't stop loving her, ⑫ _____ _____ I know I'm nothing to her. Oh, I wish there was an equation for love ⑬ _____ _____ could solve.

A Nope, there's no equation, no formula and no cure. This is something that's just outside of your scientific purview.

B So ⑭ _____ _____ I do? I'm ⑮ _____ _____ to problems I can't use my head to solve.

A You go out with me and get drunk.

Stage 2 ドラマのシーン解説

日本語訳と、解説を参照しながら、ドラマの内容を確認しよう。そのあとで、Stage1の穴埋めに再チャレンジしてみよう。

A Todd, all this scientific mumbo jumbo you're throwing ① **at her** ② **doesn't** seem to be making her heart go ③ **pitter patter**.

トッド、君が彼女に投げかけている科学的な訳のわからない呪文の数々は、彼女の胸をドキドキさせられていないようだね。

＊ mumbo jumbo「訳のわからない呪文のような言葉」　go pitter patter「ドキドキする」

B I know! I'm ④ **striking out**! ⑤ **But I** don't know ⑥ **what else** to do!

わかってるよ！　三振でアウトになりそうだよ！　でも、ほかにどうすりゃいいのかわからないんだ！

オタク・コメディー 137

* strike out「三振する」ここでは「失敗する」という意味合いで用いられている。

A Maybe it's time to face facts, Einstein.

たぶん、現実と向き合うべきときなんだよ、アインシュタイン君。

B ⑦ **And what might** those facts be?

で、その現実ってどんなものである可能性が？

* fact「事実；現実」

A She's ⑧ **not into** you. And she's NOT into science. She only pretended to be interested in BOTH subjects to ⑨ **get you to** help her with her exams.

彼女は君を好きなんかじゃないんだ。さらに、科学だって好きじゃない。両方のテーマに興味がある振りをしていただけさ。試験の手伝いを君にさせるためにね。

* pretend to be ...「…である振りをする」 subject「題目；テーマ；学科」

B You're right! You're always right. But how could she just toy with me like that? What kind of a woman ⑩ **is she**?

そのとおりだよ！ 君はいつだって正しいのさ。でも、どうして彼女は僕のことをあんなふうに弄ぶことができたんだ？ いったい彼女はどんな女なんだ？

* toy with ...「…を軽くあしらう；弄ぶ」

A She's just a woman who is way ⑪ **out of** your league, that's all. She uses guys like you because she knows you'll fall for it hook, line and sinker.

彼女は、全然、君の手が届くような女性じゃない、ただそれだけだよ。彼女は君のような男を利用するのさ。君たちがすっかりだまされてしまうって知っているからね。

* out of one's league「…に手の届かない；力の及ばない」　fall for ...「…に引っかかる；だまされる」
hook, line and sinker「すっかり；丸ごと」

B I'm sunk! I can't stop loving her, ⑫ **even though** I know I'm nothing to her. Oh, I wish there was an equation for love ⑬ **that I** could solve.

ダメだ！ 自分が彼女にとって何物でもないとわかっていても、愛することをやめられないんだ。ああ、僕に解ける愛の方程式があればいいのに。

* I'm sunk!「もうダメだ！；どうしようもない！」　equation「方程式」

A Nope, there's no equation, no formula and no cure. This is something that's just outside of your scientific purview.

いや、方程式なんてないよ。公式も治療法もね。これは単純に、君の科学的権限の外のものなのさ。

* formula「公式」　cure「治療（法）」　purview「範囲；権限；限界」

B So ⑭ **what do** I do? I'm ⑮ **not used** to problems I can't use my head to solve.

じゃあ、僕はどうすれば？ 僕は、解決に頭を使えない問題には慣れていないんだよ。

A You go out with me and get drunk.

僕と出かけて酔っ払うのさ。

* get drunk「酔っ払う」

オタク・コメディー　139

Stage 3 英文トランスクリプション

ドラマのシーン全体を英文の原稿で確認しながらCDで耳慣らししよう！ その上で、ドラマ・シーンの音声を聴きながら、まだできていない部分の穴埋めに再チャレンジしよう。

● ● ● ● ● ●

Ⓐ Todd, all this scientific mumbo jumbo you're throwing ① **at her** ② **doesn't** seem to be making her heart go ③ **pitter patter**.

Ⓑ I know! I'm ④ **striking out**! ⑤ **But I** don't know ⑥ **what else** to do!

Ⓐ Maybe it's time to face facts, Einstein.

Ⓑ ⑦ **And what might** those facts be?

Ⓐ She's ⑧ **not into** you. And she's NOT into science. She only pretended to be interested in BOTH subjects to ⑨ **get you to** help her with her exams.

Ⓑ You're right! You're always right. But how could she just toy with me like that? What kind of a woman ⑩ **is she**?

Ⓐ She's just a woman who is way ⑪ **out of** your league, that's all. She uses guys like you because she knows you'll fall for it hook, line and sinker.

Ⓑ I'm sunk! I can't stop loving her, ⑫ **even though** I know I'm nothing to her. Oh, I wish there was an equation for love ⑬ **that I** could solve.

Ⓐ Nope, there's no equation, no formula and no cure. This is something that's just outside of your scientific purview.

Ⓑ So ⑭ **what do** I do? I'm ⑮ **not used** to problems I can't use my head to solve.

Ⓐ You go out with me and get drunk.

Stage 4 音声変化をチェック

まとめとして、穴埋め部分の音声変化の特徴を**スロー・スピード**と**ナチュラル・スピード**で確認しよう。下記に示したカタカナ表記で音声変化を確認して、もう一度ドラマを聴き直してみよう。発音変化のルールは適宜復習しよう。

❶ **at her** アット・ハー ▶ アッダ [ラ] ー
☞ at に弱化した her [ァー] が連結。連結部で [t] 音が弾音化する。

❷ **doesn't** ダズント ▶ ダズン＿
☞ 末尾の破裂音 [t] が脱落する。

❸ **pitter patter** ピッター・パッター ▶ ピッダ [ラ] ーパッダ [ラ] ー
☞ 2語それぞれで破裂音 [t] が弾音化する。

❹ **striking out** ストゥライキング・アウト ▶ ストゥライキナウト
☞ striking 末尾の [g] 音が脱落しつつ、out に連結する。

❺ **But I** バット・アイ ▶ バッダ [ラ] イ
☞ 連結部で [t] 音が弾音化する。

❻ **what else** ワット・エゥス ▶ ワッデ [レ] ゥス
☞ 連結部で [t] 音が弾音化する。

❼ **And what might** アンド・ワット・マイト ▶ アン＿ワッ＿マイッ＿
☞ And, what, might それぞれの末尾で破裂音が脱落する。

❽ **not into** ナット・イントゥー ▶ ナッディ [リ] ントゥー
☞ 2語が連結する。連結部で [t] 音が弾音化する。

❾ **get you to** ゲット・ユー・トゥー ▶ ゲッチュードゥ [ル] ー
☞ get you の [t] + [j] の部分で音が混じり合い、[チュ] に近い音に変化する。to では破裂音 [t] が弾音化する。

❿ **is she** イズ・シー ▶ イッ＿シー
☞ [z] + [ʃ] の類似子音の連続で片方が脱落する。

⓫ **out of** アウト・ァヴ ▶ アウダ [ラ] ヴ
☞ 連結部で [t] 音が弾音化する。

⓬ **even though** イーヴン・ゾウ ▶ イーヴノウ
☞ [n] + [ð] が [n] 音に変化する。

⓭ **that I** ザット・アイ ▶ ザッダ [ラ] イ
☞ 連結部で [t] 音が弾音化する。

⓮ **what do** ワット・ドゥー ▶ ワッ＿ドゥー
☞ what の破裂音 [t] が脱落する。

⓯ **not used** ナット・ユースト ▶ ナッ＿ユース (ト)
☞ not の破裂音 [t] が脱落する。used 末尾の [t] 音が脱落する場合もある。

オタク・コメディー 141

Unit 23 ラブコメ

Romance Comedy (How I Met Your Mother type)

Stage 1 穴埋めドラマ・リスニング

音声変化に注意してCDでドラマの音声を聴きながら空欄部分を埋めてみよう。CDのナチュラル音声での聴き取りが難しいときは、次のトラックに収録されたスロー音声で聴いてみよう。

● ● ● ● ●

A So, dad, how ① _____ _____ _____ mom meet? And leave out the mushy stuff!

B Leave out the mushy stuff? ② _____ _____ the best part! I can't tell this story without mushy stuff.

A Okay, you can leave in a ③ _____ mushy stuff, ④ _____ _____ trigger warnings.

B What the heck is a ⑤ _____ warning?

A It means you have to tell us when the story is ⑥ _____ _____ get mushy.

B Oh, okay. So where was I? How far along ⑦ _____ _____ come?

A You just broke up ⑧ _____ _____ veterinarian, and your dog just died.

B Oh, yeah. Beverly. And Muffin. Beverly was the dog's name, by the way.

A You ⑨ _____ _____ girlfriend named Muffin?

B No, I had a girlfriend I CALLED Muffin. Should I have given a trigger warning ⑩ _____ _____?

A No, ⑪ _____ _____. Just go on with the story, PLEASE!

B Okay, so the breakup, and losing Beverly, really hit me hard. For about two months I was in a ⑫ _____ funk. I ⑬ _____ _____ my life was over.

A And then you met mom and life became worthwhile again?

B ⑭ _____ _____. Just ⑮ _____ _____ tell the story, okay? What happened was …

Stage 2 ドラマのシーン解説

日本語訳と、解説を参照しながら、ドラマの内容を確認しよう。そのあとで、Stage1の穴埋めに再チャレンジしてみよう。

A So, dad, how ① **DID you and** mom meet? And leave out the mushy stuff!

で、パパ、ママとはどうやって出会ったの？ 感傷的な部分は省いて話して！

＊ leave out ... 「…を省く；除く；除外する」　mushy「感傷的な」

B Leave out the mushy stuff? ② **But that's** the best part! I can't tell this story without mushy stuff.

感傷的な部分を除いてだって？ でも、そこがいちばんいいくだりじゃないか！ 感傷的にならずに物語は語れないよ。

ラブコメ 143

A Okay, you can leave in a ③ **little** mushy stuff, ④ **but include** trigger warnings.

わかったわ。ちょっとだけ感傷的なのも入れていいわ。でも、トリガー・ウォーニングを入れてちょうだい。

＊ trigger warning「不快を催させる一部の内容などを警告する（掲示板などの）注意書き」

B What the heck is a ⑤ **trigger** warning?

トリガー・ウォーニングって、いったいなんだ？

A It means you have to tell us when the story is ⑥ **about to** get mushy.

話が感傷的になりそうなときにそう言わなきゃダメってことよ。

＊ be about to ...「…しそうだ；…しようとするところだ」

B Oh, okay. So where was I? How far along ⑦ **have I** come?

ああ、了解。で、どこだっけ？ どこまで話したっけ？

A You just broke up ⑧ **with the** veterinarian, and your dog just died.

パパが、ちょうど獣医と別れて、パパのワンちゃんがちょうどお亡くなりになったところよ。

＊ veterinarian「獣医」

B Oh, yeah. Beverly. And Muffin. Beverly was the dog's name, by the way.

ああ、そうだ。ビバリー。それにマフィン。ちなみに、ビバリーがイヌの名前だったんだ。

＊ by the way「ついでだが；余談だが」

Ⓐ You ⑨ **had a** girlfriend named Muffin?

パパ、マフィンって名前の恋人がいたの？

Ⓑ No, I had a girlfriend I CALLED Muffin. Should I have given a trigger warning ⑩ **about that**?

いや、パパには、パパがマフィンと呼んでた恋人がいたんだよ。この件では、トリガー・ウォーニングをやっとくべきだったかな？

Ⓐ No, ⑪ **forget it**. Just go on with the story, PLEASE!

いや、忘れていいわ。ただ話を続けてちょうだいよ、お願いだから！

Ⓑ Okay, so the breakup, and losing Beverly, really hit me hard. For about two months I was in a ⑫ **total** funk. I ⑬ **felt like** my life was over.

わかったよ、で別離と、そしてビバリーを失ったことで、パパはひどくショックを受けた。約2カ月の間パパは完全に意気消沈してた。人生終わったみたいに感じてたんだ。

＊ breakup「別離」　funk「パニック状態；意気消沈」

Ⓐ And then you met mom and life became worthwhile again?

で、ママと出会って、また人生が価値あるものになったの？

Ⓑ ⑭ **Not exactly**. Just ⑮ **let me** tell the story, okay? What happened was …

ちょっと違うよ。パパに、話をさせてくれよ、いい？　なにが起こったのかというとさ…

Stage 3 英文トランスクリプション

ドラマのシーン全体を英文の原稿で確認しながらCDで耳慣らししよう！ その上で、ドラマ・シーンの音声を聴きながら、まだできていない部分の穴埋めに再チャレンジしよう。

● ● ● ● ●

A So, dad, how ① **DID you and** mom meet? And leave out the mushy stuff!

B Leave out the mushy stuff? ② **But that's** the best part! I can't tell this story without mushy stuff.

A Okay, you can leave in a ③ **little** mushy stuff, ④ **but include** trigger warnings.

B What the heck is a ⑤ **trigger** warning?

A It means you have to tell us when the story is ⑥ **about to** get mushy.

B Oh, okay. So where was I? How far along ⑦ **have I** come?

A You just broke up ⑧ **with the** veterinarian, and your dog just died.

B Oh, yeah. Beverly. And Muffin. Beverly was the dog's name, by the way.

A You ⑨ **had a** girlfriend named Muffin?

B No, I had a girlfriend I CALLED Muffin. Should I have given a trigger warning ⑩ **about that**?

A No, ⑪ **forget it**. Just go on with the story, PLEASE!

B Okay, so the breakup, and losing Beverly, really hit me hard. For about two months I was in a ⑫ **total** funk. I ⑬ **felt like** my life was over.

A And then you met mom and life became worthwhile again?

B ⑭ **Not exactly**. Just ⑮ **let me** tell the story, okay? What happened was ...

Stage 4 音声変化をチェック

まとめとして、穴埋め部分の音声変化の特徴を**スロー・スピード**と**ナチュラル・スピード**で確認しよう。下記に示したカタカナ表記で音声変化を確認して、もう一度ドラマを聴き直してみよう。発音変化のルールは適宜復習しよう。

❶ DID you and ディッド・ユー・アンド ▶ ディッジューアン＿
☞ DID you の連結部 [d] + [j] の部分で音が混じり合い、[ジュ] に近い音に変化する。and の破裂音 [d] が脱落する。

❷ But that's バット・ザッツ ▶ バッ＿ザッツ
☞ But の破裂音 [t] が脱落する。

❸ little リトゥゥ ▶ リドゥ [ル] ゥ
☞ 破裂音 [t] が弾音化する。

❹ but include バット・インクゥード ▶ バッディ [リ] ンクゥー (ド)
☞ 連結部で破裂音 [t] が弾音化する。include 末尾の [d] 音が脱落する場合もある。

❺ trigger トゥリガー ▶ チュリガー
☞ [tr] 部分の [t] 音が [チュ] に近い音に変化する。

❻ about to アバウト・トゥー ▶ アバウッ＿トゥー
☞ about 末尾の破裂音 [t] が脱落する。

❼ have I ハヴ・アイ ▶ ＿ァヴアイ
☞ have は弱化して [əv] と発話される場合がある。

❽ with the ウィズ・ザ ▶ ウィッ＿ザ
☞ [ð] 音の連続で、片方が脱落する。

❾ had a ハッド・ア ▶ ハッダ [ラ]
☞ 2語が連結。連結部で破裂音 [d] が弾音化する場合もある。

❿ about that アバウト・ザット ▶ アバウッ＿ザッ＿
☞ 2語それぞれの末尾の破裂音 [t] が脱落する。

⓫ forget it フォーゲット・イット ▶ フォーゲッディ [リ] ッ＿
☞ 連結部で [t] 音が弾音化する。it 末尾の破裂音 [t] 音も脱落しやすい。

⓬ total トウトゥゥ ▶ トウドゥ [ル] ゥ
☞ 破裂音 [t] が弾音化する。

⓭ felt like フェゥト・ライク ▶ フェゥッ＿ライク
☞ felt 末尾の破裂音 [t] が脱落する。

⓮ Not exactly ナット・エグザクトゥリー ▶ ナッデ [レ] グザク (トゥ) リー
☞ 連結部で [t] 音が弾音化する。exactly の破裂音 [t] 音も脱落しやすい。

⓯ let me レット・ミー ▶ レッ＿ミー
☞ let の破裂音 [t] 音が脱落する。

ラブコメ 147

Unit 24 セクシー・ミステリー・ドラマ
Sex/Mystery Drama (Desperate Housewives type)

Stage 1 穴埋めドラマ・リスニング

音声変化に注意してCDでドラマの音声を聴きながら空欄部分を埋めてみよう。CDのナチュラル音声での聴き取りが難しいときは、次のトラックに収録されたスロー音声で聴いてみよう。

● ● ● ● ●

A So, who is your husband sleeping ① _____ _____ days?

B As if I care! I'm just glad ② _____ _____ me!

A You're ③ _____ _____ curious? Or jealous?

B I'm over all that. Anyway, WHOEVER ④ _____ _____, she's finding ⑤ _____ _____ that Clarence is a lousy screw.

A Wow, who'da thought? He seems like Mr. Debonair and Dashing.

B Oh he pours on the charm all right. I'll ⑥ _____ _____ that. ⑦ _____ _____ fell for it. ⑧ _____ _____ turns the bedroom into the 'bored room.'

A Hmmm ... Anyway, who do you think is ⑨ _____ _____ blackmail him?

B I don't know! I've had my suspicions for a while now ⑩ _____ _____ involved with some shady characters. I just don't know ⑪ _____ _____ _____ up to. But I intend to find out.

A So, are you thinking of hiring a ⑫ _____ _____?

B I already have. I ⑬ _____ _____, I don't ⑭ _____ _____ know anything about my husband's affairs. But I want the goods on everything ELSE he's mixed up in.

A Oh, my God. I really hope ⑮ _____ _____ _____ any kind of danger, Lynette.

B I feel really uneasy, to tell you the truth. Deep down, I'm not such a tough cookie.

Stage 2 ドラマのシーン解説

日本語訳と、解説を参照しながら、ドラマの内容を確認しよう。そのあとで、Stage1の穴埋めに再チャレンジしてみよう。

A So, who is your husband sleeping ① **with these** days?

で、あなたのダンナは、最近だれと寝てるのよ？

B As if I care! I'm just glad ② **it isn't** me!

私はまったく気にしてないんだからね！ 私じゃなくて清清してるの！

* As if I care!「私が気にしているみたいに (言うのはやめて)！；知ったことか！」

A You're ③ **not even** curious? Or jealous?

興味もないってわけ？ あるいは嫉妬も？

B I'm over all that. Anyway, WHOEVER ④ **it is**, she's finding ⑤ **out now** that Clarence is a lousy screw.

全然。とにかく、それがだれであっても、いまごろはクラレンスがひどいセックス下手だって理解している頃よ。

＊ be over「乗り越える」　lousy「ひどい」　screw「セックスの相手」

A Wow, who'da thought? He seems like Mr. Debonair and Dashing.

うわっ、想像もできないわ。彼って、やさしくってカッコいい男性の見本みたいに見えるもの。

＊ who'da thought? = who would have thought?「だれがそんなことを思ったでしょう＝だれもそんなことちっとも思いはしなかった」　debonair「しゃれた；粋な；スマートで親切な」
dashing「カッコいい；魅力的な」

B Oh he pours on the charm all right. I'll ⑥ **give him** that. ⑦ **And I** fell for it. ⑧ **But he** turns the bedroom into the 'bored room.'

ああ、彼は上手に呪文をかけるのよ。その才能は認めるわ。そして、私はそれにやられちゃったの。でもね、彼はベッド・ルームを退屈な部屋に変えちゃうのよ。

＊ pours on「浴びせる」　charm「呪文」　all right「確かに；ちゃんと」
give ... that「それについて…を認める」　fall for ...「…に引っかかる」

A Hmmm ... Anyway, who do you think is ⑨ **trying to** blackmail him?

ふーん…それはさておき、あなたは、だれが彼を恐喝してると思うの？

＊ blackmail「恐喝する；脅す」

B I don't know! I've had my suspicions for a while now ⑩ **that he's** involved with some shady characters. I just don't know ⑪ **what he's been** up to. But I intend to find out.

知らないわよ！　このところ、ずっと彼が怪しい連中とつき合ってるんじゃないかって疑いは

もってたの。彼がずっと、なにをやっているのかは、わからないわ。でも、探り出すつもりよ。

* for a while now「このところしばらく」 shady character「怪しい人物」
be up to ...「…をして；…しようとして」

A So, are you thinking of hiring a ⑫ **private detective**?

ということは、私立探偵を雇おうと思ってるの？

* private detective「私立探偵」

B I already have. I ⑬ **told him**, I don't ⑭ **want to** know anything about my husband's affairs. But I want the goods on everything ELSE he's mixed up in.

すでに依頼したわ。探偵には夫の情事についてはなにも知りたくないと言ったの。でも、彼が巻き込まれているほかのことに関する証拠は全部、欲しいってね。

* goods「犯罪の証拠」 be mixed up in ...「…に巻き込まれている」

A Oh, my God. I really hope ⑮ **you're not in** any kind of danger, Lynette.

なんてこと。あなたが危険なことに巻き込まれないように心から祈ってるわ、リネット。

B I feel really uneasy, to tell you the truth. Deep down, I'm not such a tough cookie.

私はすごく不安なの、本音を言えばね。内心、私はそんなにタフじゃないのよ。

* to tell you the truth「本音を言うと」 deep down「内心は」 tough cookie「タフな人」

セクシー・ミステリー・ドラマ 151

Stage 3 英文トランスクリプション

ドラマのシーン全体を英文の原稿で確認しながらCDで耳慣らししよう！ その上で、ドラマ・シーンの音声を聴きながら、まだできていない部分の穴埋めに再チャレンジしよう。

● ● ● ● ● ●

A So, who is your husband sleeping ① **with these** days?

B As if I care! I'm just glad ② **it isn't** me!

A You're ③ **not even** curious? Or jealous?

B I'm over all that. Anyway, WHOEVER ④ **it is**, she's finding ⑤ **out now** that Clarence is a lousy screw.

A Wow, who'da thought? He seems like Mr. Debonair and Dashing.

B Oh he pours on the charm all right. I'll ⑥ **give him** that. ⑦ **And I** fell for it. ⑧ **But he** turns the bedroom into the 'bored room.'

A Hmmm ... Anyway, who do you think is ⑨ **trying to** blackmail him?

B I don't know! I've had my suspicions for a while now ⑩ **that he's** involved with some shady characters. I just don't know ⑪ **what he's been** up to. But I intend to find out.

A So, are you thinking of hiring a ⑫ **private detective**?

B I already have. I ⑬ **told him**, I don't ⑭ **want to** know anything about my husband's affairs. But I want the goods on everything ELSE he's mixed up in.

A Oh, my God. I really hope ⑮ **you're not in** any kind of danger, Lynette.

B I feel really uneasy, to tell you the truth. Deep down, I'm not such a tough cookie.

Stage 4 音声変化をチェック

まとめとして、穴埋め部分の音声変化の特徴を**スロー・スピード**と**ナチュラル・スピード**で確認しよう。下記に示したカタカナ表記で音声変化を確認して、もう一度ドラマを聴き直してみよう。発音変化のルールは適宜復習しよう。

❶ **with these**　　　　　　　　ウィズ・ズィーズ　　　　▶ ウィッ＿ズィーズ
☞ [ð] 音の連続で、片方が脱落する。

❷ **it isn't**　　　　　　　　　　イット・イズント　　　　▶ イッディ[リ] ズン＿
☞ 2語が連結。連結部で破裂音 [t] が弾音化する。isn't 末尾の破裂音 [t] が脱落する。

❸ **not even**　　　　　　　　　ナット・イーヴン　　　　▶ ナッディ[リ] ーヴン
☞ 連結部で [t] 音が弾音化する。

❹ **it is**　　　　　　　　　　　イット・イズ　　　　　　▶ イッディ[リ] ズ
☞ 連結部で [t] 音が弾音化する。

❺ **out now**　　　　　　　　　アウト・ナウ　　　　　　▶ アウッ＿ナウ
☞ out 末尾の破裂音 [t] が脱落する。

❻ **give him**　　　　　　　　　ギヴ・ヒム　　　　　　　▶ ギヴィム
☞ give が弱化した him [イム] に連結する。

❼ **And I**　　　　　　　　　　アンド・アイ　　　　　　▶ アナイ
☞ And の [d] 音が脱落しつつ、I に連結する。

❽ **But he**　　　　　　　　　　バット・ヒー　　　　　　▶ バッディ[リ] ー
☞ But が弱化した he [イー] に連結する。連結部で破裂音 [t] が弾音化する。

❾ **trying to**　　　　　　　　　トゥライイング・トゥー　　▶ チュライン＿トゥー
☞ [tr] の [t] 音は [チュ] のように変化する。破裂音 [g] は脱落しやすい。

❿ **that he's**　　　　　　　　　ザット・ヒーズ　　　　　▶ ザッディ[リ] ーズ
☞ that が弱化した he's [イーズ] に連結。連結部で破裂音 [t] が弾音化する。

⓫ **what he's been**　　　　　　ワット・ヒーズ・ビーン　　▶ ワッディ[リ] ズビン
☞ he's は [イズ]、been は [ビン] と弱化。what he's の連結部で破裂音 [t] が弾音化する。

⓬ **private detective**　　　　　プライヴィット・ディテクティヴ
　　　　　　　　　　　　　　　　　　　　　　　　　　　▶ プライヴィッ＿ディテ(ク)ティヴ
☞ private 末尾の [t] 音や detective の [k] 音は脱落しやすい。

⓭ **told him**　　　　　　　　　トウゥド・ヒム　　　　　▶ トウゥディ[リ] ム
☞ told が弱化した him [イム] に連結。連結部で破裂音 [t] が弾音化する。

⓮ **want to**　　　　　　　　　ワント・トゥー　　　　　▶ ワナ
☞ want の破裂音 [t] が脱落し、弱化した to [ア] に連結する。

⓯ **you're not in**　　　　　　　ユアー・ナット・イン　　　▶ ユアナッディ[リ] ン
☞ you're は短く [ユア] と発話。not in の連結部で破裂音 [t] が弾音化する。

セクシー・ミステリー・ドラマ　153

Unit 25 犯罪ドラマ
Crime Drama (Breaking Bad type)

Stage 1 穴埋めドラマ・リスニング

音声変化に注意してCDでドラマの音声を聴きながら空欄部分を埋めてみよう。CDのナチュラル音声での聴き取りが難しいときは、次のトラックに収録されたスロー音声で聴いてみよう。

● ● ● ● ● ●

A Look, you're involved with some really dangerous characters. You do realize that, ① _____ _____?

B Yeah, ② _____ _____ also realize that no less than three doctors give me six months to live. And the last I heard, you can only die once.

A It's not just ③ _____ _____, you idiot. These guys … if you cross them … they'll come after your family. You HAVE ④ _____ _____ _____, haven't you?

B Of course. That's why I ⑤ _____ _____ _____ cross them.

A You have no idea ⑥ _____ you're involved in. That's plain as day. These guys, at some point, they will ⑦ _____ _____ to do things you can't possibly justify doing. ⑧ _____ _____, you WILL cross them.

B ⑨ _____ _____ first got involved in this, I had only one purpose in mind. To use the little time I have left so that my family ⑩ _____ go hungry after I'm gone.

Ⓐ And ⑪ _____ _____ now?

Ⓑ Nothing has changed. That's my one, ⑫ _____ _____, purpose. I'm ⑬ _____ _____ _____ ⑭ _____ _____ people I am working with now may require of me at some point. I've made my choice.

Ⓐ Then God help you, brother. Because you are ⑮ _____ _____ die with a VERY guilty conscience.

Stage 2 ドラマのシーン解説

日本語訳と、解説を参照しながら、ドラマの内容を確認しよう。そのあとで、Stage1の穴埋めに再チャレンジしてみよう。

Ⓐ Look, you're involved with some really dangerous characters. You do realize that, ① **don't you**?

いいか、お前はとても危険な奴らと関わっているんだ。そのことに気づいているんだよな？

＊ be involved with ... 「…と関わっている」

Ⓑ Yeah, ② **and I** also realize that no less than three doctors give me six months to live. And the last I heard, you can only die once.

ああ、それに3人もの医者が俺に余命6カ月と宣言していることにもね。それに、最近、聞いたところでは、人間は一度しか死ねないんだそうだ。

犯罪ドラマ 155

＊ no less than ... 「…も」　the last I heard, ... 「この前聞いたところでは…」

Ⓐ It's not just ③ **about you**, you idiot. These guys ... if you cross them ... they'll come after your family. You HAVE ④ **thought about that**, haven't you?

お前だけの話じゃないんだよ、バカ野郎。あいつらはさ…もしお前が裏切れば…君の家族を追ってくる。そのことについては、考えたことがあるのかよ？

＊ cross「裏切る；逆らう」　come after ...「追ってくる」

Ⓑ Of course. That's why I ⑤ **don't intend to** cross them.

もちろんだ。だから、俺は奴らを裏切るつもりなどないのさ。

＊ intend to ...「…するつもりだ」

Ⓐ You have no idea ⑥ **what** you're involved in. That's plain as day. These guys, at some point, they will ⑦ **want you** to do things you can't possibly justify doing. ⑧ **And then**, you WILL cross them.

お前は、自分がなにに巻き込まれているのかわかってないんだよ。明白なことだ。ある時点で奴らは、お前にはどうしても正当化できない行為をさせたがるだろう。そして、お前は、きっと奴らを裏切ることになるんだよ。

＊ plain as day「極めて明白な」　possibly「どうあっても…（ない）」　justify「正当化する」

Ⓑ ⑨ **When I** first got involved in this, I had only one purpose in mind. To use the little time I have left so that my family ⑩ **won't** go hungry after I'm gone.

俺が最初にこの件に関わったときに、頭の中にはたったひとつの目的しかなかった。俺がいなくなったあとで家族が腹を空かせないように、自分に残されたわずかな時間を使うことさ。

＊ purpose「目的」　go hungry「飢える」　be gone「死ぬ」

Ⓐ And ⑪ **how about** now?

で、いまはどうなんだ？

Ⓑ Nothing has changed. That's my one, ⑫ **and only**, purpose. I'm ⑬ **not bothered about** ⑭ **what the** people I am working with now may require of me at some point. I've made my choice.

なにも変わっちゃいないさ。それこそ、俺のたったひとつの目的なんだ。ある時点で、いま俺が関わっている人間が俺になにを要求するかなんて知ったことか。俺は選択したんだよ。

* one and only「たったひとつの；唯一無二の」 be bothered about ...「…に心を配る」
  require of ...「…に要求する」

Ⓐ Then God help you, brother. Because you are ⑮ **going to** die with a VERY guilty conscience.

だとすれば、かわいそうなことだ、兄弟。お前は、ひどい罪の意識とともに死んでいくことになるんだからな。

* God help you.「大変なことだ；かわいそうなことだ」 guilty conscience「自責の念」

Stage 3 英文トランスクリプション

ドラマのシーン全体を英文の原稿で確認しながらCDで耳慣らししよう！ その上で、ドラマ・シーンの音声を聴きながら、まだできていない部分の穴埋めに再チャレンジしよう。

● ● ● ● ●

A Look, you're involved with some really dangerous characters. You do realize that, ① **don't you**?

B Yeah, ② **and I** also realize that no less than three doctors give me six months to live. And the last I heard, you can only die once.

A It's not just ③ **about you**, you idiot. These guys ... if you cross them ... they'll come after your family. You HAVE ④ **thought about that**, haven't you?

B Of course. That's why I ⑤ **don't intend to** cross them.

A You have no idea ⑥ **what** you're involved in. That's plain as day. These guys, at some point, they will ⑦ **want you** to do things you can't possibly justify doing. ⑧ **And then**, you WILL cross them.

B ⑨ **When I** first got involved in this, I had only one purpose in mind. To use the little time I have left so that my family ⑩ **won't** go hungry after I'm gone.

A And ⑪ **how about** now?

B Nothing has changed. That's my one, ⑫ **and only**, purpose. I'm ⑬ **not bothered about** ⑭ **what the** people I am working with now may require of me at some point. I've made my choice.

A Then God help you, brother. Because you are ⑮ **going to** die with a VERY guilty conscience.

Stage 4 音声変化をチェック

まとめとして、穴埋め部分の音声変化の特徴を**スロー・スピード**と**ナチュラル・スピード**で確認しよう。下記に示したカタカナ表記で音声変化を確認して、もう一度ドラマを聴き直してみよう。発音変化のルールは適宜復習しよう。

❶ **don't you** ドウント・ユー ▶ ドン＿ユ
☞ don't は弱化。don't 末尾の [t] 音が脱落する。

❷ **and I** アンド・アイ ▶ アナイ
☞ and の破裂音 [d] が脱落しつつ、I に連結する。

❸ **about you** アバウト・ユー ▶ アバウッ＿ユー
☞ about 末尾の破裂音 [t] が脱落する。

❹ **thought about that** ソート・アバウト・ザット ▶ ソーダ [ラ] バウッ＿ザッ＿
☞ thought about の連結部で破裂音 [t] が弾音化する。about や that 末尾の [t] 音も脱落する。

❺ **don't intend to** ドウント・インテンド・トゥー
▶ ドン＿インテン＿ドゥ [ル] ー
☞ 弱化した don't や intend 末尾の破裂音が脱落する。to の破裂音 [t] が弾音化する。

❻ **what** ワット ▶ ワッ＿
☞ 末尾の破裂音 [t] が脱落する。

❼ **want you** ワント・ユー ▶ ワン＿ユー
☞ want 末尾の破裂音 [t] が脱落する。

❽ **And then** アンド・ゼン ▶ アン＿ゼン
☞ And 末尾の破裂音 [d] が脱落する。

❾ **When I** ウェン・アイ ▶ ウェナイ
☞ 2 語が連結する。

❿ **won't** ウォウント ▶ ウォウン＿
☞ 末尾の破裂音 [t] が脱落する。

⓫ **how about** ハウ・アバウト ▶ ハウ＿バウッ＿
☞ about の頭の [ə] 音と末尾の破裂音 [t] が脱落する。

⓬ **and only** アンド・オウンリー ▶ アノウンリー
☞ and 末尾の破裂音 [d] が脱落しつつ、2 語が連結する。

⓭ **not bothered about** ナット・バザード・アバウト ▶ ナッ＿バザーダバウッ＿
☞ bothered about は連結。not と about 末尾の破裂音 [t] が脱落する。

⓮ **what the** ワット・ザ ▶ ワッ＿ザ
☞ what 末尾の破裂音 [t] が脱落する。

⓯ **going to** ゴウイング・トゥー ▶ ゴウイン＿トゥー
☞ going 末尾の破裂音 [g] が脱落する。

犯罪ドラマ 159

Unit 26 広告業界ドラマ
Advertising Industry Drama (Mad Men type)

Stage 1　穴埋めドラマ・リスニング

音声変化に注意してCDでドラマの音声を聴きながら空欄部分を埋めてみよう。CDのナチュラル音声での聴き取りが難しいときは、次のトラックに収録されたスロー音声で聴いてみよう。

● ● ● ● ●

A Have you ever ① _____ _____ Edward Bernays?

B Can't say ② _____ _____ have. Should I have?

A ③ _____ necessarily. His uncle is a ④ _____ more famous. Sigmund Freud.

B Uh, yeah. Him I know. So who is this Edward guy, besides being Sigmund Freud's nephew?

A Well, he used his uncle's ideas, basically, to do ⑤ _____ _____ do. To sell bacon, cigarettes, soap, coffee, you name it. He ⑥ _____ _____ that to make people HAVE to have something, you have to reach them ⑦ _____ _____ levels.

B So we're all psychologists; is that ⑧ _____ _____ saying?

A The best of us are. ⑨ _____ _____ you think we were doing?

B I guess I didn't think ⑩ _____ _____ ⑪ _____ _____. So, ⑫ _____ _____ study this Bernays guy?

160

A You don't have to. You just ⑬ _____ _____ know that every man, woman and child has really deep longings and needs that can never be fulfilled. BUT, they can be ⑭ _____, for one brief moment, into thinking they can.

B ⑮ _____ makes it sound so manipulative. Like all of us in this industry are just a bunch of con men ... and women.

A Well, if the shoe fits ... buy it.

Stage 2 ドラマのシーン解説

日本語訳と、解説を参照しながら、ドラマの内容を確認しよう。そのあとで、Stage1の穴埋めに再チャレンジしてみよう。

A Have you ever ① **heard of** Edward Bernays?

エドワード・バーネイズのことは聞いたことある?

B Can't say ② **that I** have. Should I have?

聞いたことがあるとは言えないわ。知ってるべきなの?

A ③ **Not** necessarily. His uncle is a ④ **bit** more famous. Sigmund Freud.

そうでもないけどね。彼のおじさんはもうちょっと有名なんだ。ジークムント・フロイトさ。

B Uh, yeah. Him I know. So who is this Edward guy, besides being Sigmund Freud's nephew?

あ、そうか。彼なら知ってるわ。で、このエドワードなんとかって人はだれなの？ ジークムント・フロイトの甥っ子であること以外に？

* besides ... 「…を除いて」

A Well, he used his uncle's ideas, basically, to do ⑤ **what we** do. To sell bacon, cigarettes, soap, coffee, you name it. He ⑥ **figured out** that to make people HAVE to have something, you have to reach them ⑦ **at deeper** levels.

あのね、基本的には、彼はおじさんのアイデアを使ったんだよ、僕らのやっていることをやるのにね。ベーコンや、タバコ、石けん、コーヒー、なんでもいいけど販売するためにさ。人間になにかを所有しなきゃと思わせるのには、その人たちに深いレベルでコンタクトしなきゃならないという答えを彼は見つけ出したんだよ。

* ... you name it 「…など、どんなものでも；なんでも」　figure out 「答えを導く；考え出す」

B So we're all psychologists; is that ⑧ **what you're** saying?

ということは、私たちはみんな精神分析医よね、そう言いたいの？

* psychologist 「精神分析医；心理学者」

A The best of us are. ⑨ **What did** you think we were doing?

僕らの中でも最高の人たちはね。君は、僕らがなにをしていると思ってた？

B I guess I didn't think ⑩ **that much** ⑪ **about it**. So, ⑫ **should I** study this Bernays guy?

さあ、あまり考えたことはなかったわ。で、私はこのバーネイズっていう人のことを勉強すべきなのかなぁ？

A You don't have to. You just ⑬ **need to** know that every man, woman and child has really deep longings and needs that can never be fulfilled. BUT, they can be ⑭ **tricked**, for one brief moment, into thinking they can.

その必要はないよ。あらゆる男性や女性、子どもは、心の深いところに、決して満たされることのない渇望やニーズを抱いているってことを知っているだけでいいよ。でもね、彼らはちょっとした瞬間にトリックにかかるのさ。そして、それを満たすことができると思っちゃうんだよ。

* longing「強い願望」 need「必要性；ニーズ」 fulfill「満たす」

B ⑮ **That** makes it sound so manipulative. Like all of us in this industry are just a bunch of con men ... and women.

ものすごくまやかしっぽく聞こえるわね。この業界の私たちみんなが、詐欺師の集まりみたいじゃない。

* manipulative「操作的な；ごまかしの」 bunch「集まり；一味」 con man「ペテン師；詐欺師」

A Well, if the shoe fits ... buy it.

ああ、そう思うんなら、そうなんだろうさ。

* If the shoe fits(, wear/buy it).「もし思い当たるところがあるなら、おそらくそうなのだろう」通常は wear it を使う。シニカルな表現。

Stage 3 英文トランスクリプション

ドラマのシーン全体を英文の原稿で確認しながらCDで耳慣らししよう！ その上で、ドラマ・シーンの音声を聴きながら、まだできていない部分の穴埋めに再チャレンジしよう。

● ● ● ● ● ●

A Have you ever ① **heard of** Edward Bernays?

B Can't say ② **that I** have. Should I have?

A ③ **Not** necessarily. His uncle is a ④ **bit** more famous. Sigmund Freud.

B Uh, yeah. Him I know. So who is this Edward guy, besides being Sigmund Freud's nephew?

A Well, he used his uncle's ideas, basically, to do ⑤ **what we** do. To sell bacon, cigarettes, soap, coffee, you name it. He ⑥ **figured out** that to make people HAVE to have something, you have to reach them ⑦ **at deeper** levels.

B So we're all psychologists; is that ⑧ **what you're** saying?

A The best of us are. ⑨ **What did** you think we were doing?

B I guess I didn't think ⑩ **that much** ⑪ **about it**. So, ⑫ **should I** study this Bernays guy?

A You don't have to. You just ⑬ **need to** know that every man, woman and child has really deep longings and needs that can never be fulfilled. BUT, they can be ⑭ **tricked**, for one brief moment, into thinking they can.

B ⑮ **That** makes it sound so manipulative. Like all of us in this industry are just a bunch of con men ... and women.

A Well, if the shoe fits ... buy it.

Stage 4 音声変化をチェック

まとめとして、穴埋め部分の音声変化の特徴を**スロー・スピード**と**ナチュラル・スピード**で確認しよう。下記に示したカタカナ表記で音声変化を確認して、もう一度ドラマを聴き直してみよう。発音変化のルールは適宜復習しよう。

❶ **heard of** ハード・アヴ ▶ ハーダ [ラ] ヴ
☞ 連結部で破裂音 [t] が弾音化する。

❷ **that I** ザット・アイ ▶ ザッダ [ラ] イ
☞ 連結部で破裂音 [t] が弾音化する。

❸ **Not** ナット ▶ ナッ＿
☞ 末尾の破裂音 [t] が脱落する。

❹ **bit** ビット ▶ ビッ＿
☞ 末尾の破裂音 [t] が脱落する。

❺ **what we** ワット・ウィ ▶ ワッ＿ウィ
☞ what 末尾の破裂音 [t] が脱落する。

❻ **figured out** フィギャード・アウト ▶ フィギャーダウッ＿
☞ 2語が連結。out 末尾の破裂音 [t] が脱落する。

❼ **at deeper** アット・ディーパー ▶ アッ＿ディーパー
☞ at 末尾の破裂音 [t] が脱落する。

❽ **what you're** ワット・ユアー ▶ ワッチュアー
☞ [t] + [j] の部分で音が混じり合い、[チュ] に近い音に変化する。

❾ **What did** ワット・ディッド ▶ ワッ＿ディッ (ド)
☞ それぞれの語の末尾から破裂音が脱落しやすい。

❿ **that much** ザット・マッチ ▶ ザッ＿マッチ
☞ that 末尾の破裂音 [t] が脱落する。

⓫ **about it** アバウト・イット ▶ アバウディ [リ] ッ＿
☞ 連結部で [t] 音が弾音化する。it 末尾の破裂音 [t] が脱落する。

⓬ **should I** シュッド・アイ ▶ シュッダ [ラ] イ
☞ 連結部で [t] 音が弾音化する。

⓭ **need to** ニード・トゥー ▶ ニーッ＿ドゥ [ル] ー
☞ need 末尾の破裂音 [d] が脱落する。to の破裂音 [t] は弾音化する場合がある。

⓮ **tricked** トゥリックト ▶ チュリックト
☞ [tr] の [t] 音は [チュ] のように変化する。

⓯ **That** ザット ▶ ザッ＿
☞ 末尾の破裂音 [t] が脱落する。

広告業界ドラマ

Unit 27 超常現象ドラマ
Paranormal Drama (X-Files type)

Stage 1 穴埋めドラマ・リスニング

音声変化に注意してCDでドラマの音声を聴きながら空欄部分を埋めてみよう。CDのナチュラル音声での聴き取りが難しいときは、次のトラックに収録されたスロー音声で聴いてみよう。

● ● ● ● ● ●

A The file is officially closed, of course. The U.S. Navy classifies ① _____ _____ a disappearance at sea, no survivors.

B But there WERE survivors. All crew members of that flight resurfaced ten years ② _____, with unbelievable stories, ③ _____?

A Yes, a ④ _____ _____ TOO unbelievable. Each one of them was placed in a different mental institution. Their stories, ⑤ _____ _____ claimed identities, were diagnosed as 'hallucinations.' And they were ⑥ _____ no access, either to each other, or to the outside world.

B What really happened? ⑦ _____ _____ _____ discovered?

A The Navy was testing some really sophisticated aircraft ⑧ _____ _____ days. They ⑨ _____ _____ see just how high ⑩ _____ the stratosphere a manned craft could go. This one was up around ⑪ _____ five, eighty thousand feet.

B Wow! That high, in the 1930s? And in an airplane, ⑫ _____ _____ balloon?

A Yeah, the science was incredible then. The 'official' stories don't tell you the half of it.

B So, what happened up there? Did they ⑬ _____ an alien aircraft?

A No, they encountered a wormhole. They ended up in a completely different solar system, a ⑭ _____ different part of the galaxy.

B Oh my God! That's incredible! How did they ⑮ _____ _____ back?

A THAT's where the story becomes incredible …

Stage 2　ドラマのシーン解説

日本語訳と、解説を参照しながら、ドラマの内容を確認しよう。そのあとで、Stage1の穴埋めに再チャレンジしてみよう。

A The file is officially closed, of course. The U.S. Navy classifies ① **it as** a disappearance at sea, no survivors.

もちろん、この件は正式には片がついている。米国海軍は、この件を海域での失踪で、生存者なしとしているんだよ。

＊ the file is closed「事件の捜査が終了している」　classify A as B「AをBと分類する」

B But there WERE survivors. All crew members of that flight resurfaced ten years ② **later**, with unbelievable stories, ③ **right**?

しかし、生存者がいたんですね。そのフライトの全搭乗員が10年後によみがえったんですよね？　信じられないストーリーを抱えて。

超常現象ドラマ　167

* resurface「よみがえる；復活する；再浮上する」

Ⓐ Yes, a ④ **little bit** TOO unbelievable. Each one of them was placed in a different mental institution. Their stories, ⑤ **and their** claimed identities, were diagnosed as 'hallucinations.' And they were ⑥ **permitted** no access, either to each other, or to the outside world.

ああ、ちょっとあまりにも信じられないことだがね。全員が別々の精神科病院に入れられていたんだ。彼らの話や、彼らの主張する身元は「妄想」と診断された。そして、彼らは一切の接触を認められなかった、お互い同士の面会も、外の世界との接触も。

* mental institution「精神科病院」 diagnose as ...「…と診断する」 hallucination「妄想」
be permitted no access「一切の接触・面会を認められない」

Ⓑ What really happened? ⑦ **What have you** discovered?

実際なにが起こったんでしょうか？ あなたはなにを見つけたんです？

Ⓐ The Navy was testing some really sophisticated aircraft ⑧ **in those** days. They ⑨ **wanted to** see just how high ⑩ **into** the stratosphere a manned craft could go. This one was up around ⑪ **seventy** five, eighty thousand feet.

当時、海軍は非常に高度な航空機をテストしていたんだ。彼らは、人間を乗せた航空機が成層圏のどのくらいの高さまで行けるのかを知りたかったのだ。この（事件の）機体は、7万5千か、8万フィートくらいまで到達した。

* sophisticated「（技術などが）高度な」 stratosphere「成層圏」

Ⓑ Wow! That high, in the 1930s? And in an airplane, ⑫ **not a** balloon?

ええっ！ そんな高さまで、1930年代にですか？ それに、バルーンではなくて、航空機で？

A Yeah, the science was incredible then. The 'official' stories don't tell you the half of it.

ああ、当時の科学はすばらしいものだったんだ。表向きの話では、内容の半分も伝わらないんだ。

* incredible「すばらしい」 official「表向きの；公の；正式の」

B So, what happened up there? Did they ⑬ **encounter** an alien aircraft?

で、上空ではなにが起こったんです？ エイリアンの航空機にでも遭遇したんですか？

* encounter「遭遇する」

A No, they encountered a wormhole. They ended up in a completely different solar system, a ⑭ **completely** different part of the galaxy.

いや、彼らはワームホールに遭遇したんだ。結局、宇宙のまったく別の部分にあるまったく別の太陽系にたどり着いたんだ。

* end up in ...「結局…で終わる」

B Oh my God! That's incredible! How did they ⑮ **make it** back?

なんてことでしょう！ 信じられないわ！ 彼らはどうやって帰還したんです？

* make it back「なんとかして戻る」

A THAT's where the story becomes incredible ...

そこから、話が信じがたいものになるんだが…

超常現象ドラマ 169

Stage 3 英文トランスクリプション

ドラマのシーン全体を英文の原稿で確認しながらCDで耳慣らししよう！ その上で、ドラマ・シーンの音声を聴きながら、まだできていない部分の穴埋めに再チャレンジしよう。

● ● ● ● ● ●

A The file is officially closed, of course. The U.S. Navy classifies ① **it as** a disappearance at sea, no survivors.

B But there WERE survivors. All crew members of that flight resurfaced ten years ② **later**, with unbelievable stories, ③ **right**?

A Yes, a ④ **little bit** TOO unbelievable. Each one of them was placed in a different mental institution. Their stories, ⑤ **and their** claimed identities, were diagnosed as 'hallucinations.' And they were ⑥ **permitted** no access, either to each other, or to the outside world.

B What really happened? ⑦ **What have you** discovered?

A The Navy was testing some really sophisticated aircraft ⑧ **in those** days. They ⑨ **wanted to** see just how high ⑩ **into** the stratosphere a manned craft could go. This one was up around ⑪ **seventy** five, eighty thousand feet.

B Wow! That high, in the 1930s? And in an airplane, ⑫ **not a** balloon?

A Yeah, the science was incredible then. The 'official' stories don't tell you the half of it.

B So, what happened up there? Did they ⑬ **encounter** an alien aircraft?

A No, they encountered a wormhole. They ended up in a completely different solar system, a ⑭ **completely** different part of the galaxy.

B Oh my God! That's incredible! How did they ⑮ **make it** back?

A THAT's where the story becomes incredible ...

Stage 4 音声変化をチェック

まとめとして、穴埋め部分の音声変化の特徴を**スロー・スピード**と**ナチュラル・スピード**で確認しよう。下記に示したカタカナ表記で音声変化を確認して、もう一度ドラマを聴き直してみよう。発音変化のルールは適宜復習しよう。

❶ it as イット・アズ ▶ イッダ [ラ] ズ
☞ 連結部で [t] 音が弾音化する。

❷ later レイター ▶ レイダ [ラ] ー
☞ 破裂音 [t] が弾音化する。

❸ right ライト ▶ ライッ＿
☞ 末尾の破裂音 [t] が脱落する。

❹ little bit リトゥゥ・ビット ▶ リドゥ [ル] ゥビッ＿
☞ little の破裂音 [t] が弾音化する。bit 末尾の [t] 音は脱落する。

❺ and their アンド・ゼア ▶ アネア
☞ and の [d] 音が脱落しつつ、2語が連結。連結部の [n] + [ð] が [n] 音に変化する。

❻ permitted パーミッティッド ▶ パーミッディ [リ] ッ＿
☞ 破裂音 [t] が弾音化する。末尾の [d] 音は脱落する。

❼ What have you ワット・ハヴ・ユー ▶ ワッダ [ラ] ヴユー
☞ What に弱化した have [ァヴ] が連結。連結部で [t] 音が弾音化する。

❽ in those イン・ゾウズ ▶ イノウズ
☞ [n] + [ð] が [n] 音に変化する。

❾ wanted to ワンティッド・トゥー ▶ ワニッ＿ドゥ [ル] ー
☞ want から破裂音 [t] や [d] が脱落する。to の [t] 音は弾音化。

❿ into イントゥー ▶ イヌー
☞ [nt] で [t] 音の脱落が生じる。

⓫ seventy セヴンティー ▶ セヴニー
☞ [nt] で [t] 音の脱落が生じる。

⓬ not a ナット・ア ▶ ナッダ [ラ]
☞ 連結部で破裂音 [t] が弾音化する。

⓭ encounter エンカウンター ▶ エンカウナー
☞ [nt] で [t] 音の脱落が生じる。

⓮ completely カムプリートゥリー ▶ カムプリーッ＿リー
☞ [tl] で [t] 音の脱落が生じる。

⓯ make it メイク・イット ▶ メイッキッ＿
☞ 2語が連結する。it 末尾の破裂音 [t] は脱落する。

超常現象ドラマ 171

Unit 28 スーパーヒーロー・ドラマ
Superhero Drama (Smallville type)

Stage 1 穴埋めドラマ・リスニング

音声変化に注意してCDでドラマの音声を聴きながら空欄部分を埋めてみよう。CDのナチュラル音声での聴き取りが難しいときは、次のトラックに収録されたスロー音声で聴いてみよう。

● ● ● ● ● ●

A Lois, do you plan to ... I mean, ① _____ anyone asked you ...

B Clark, ② _____ _____ _____, will you? Gosh!

A Are you ③ _____ _____ the prom?

B Well, of course, I am! Everybody's going! ④ _____ _____ a blast!

A Oh, so then, you already have a date, huh?

B Well, ⑤ _____ _____. I mean, he ⑥ _____ _____ _____ yet. ⑦ _____ _____ know he's going to ...

A I see. Uhm, okay. That's all I ⑧ _____ _____ know. Uh, see ya, I guess ...

B How ⑨ _____ _____, Clark? Who are you taking?

A I, to be honest, I haven't ⑩ _____ anyone yet. I mean, I was going to. That is, I was planning to ask ... you.

B Oh, Clark! ⑪ _____ be silly! You know there's only one fella for me!

172

A Superguy? You're ⑫ _____ for Superguy to ask you to the prom?

B Sure I am! He's my steady, after all!

A Lois, he's a superhero! I'm ⑬ _____ sure he has more important things to do than take a girl to the prom!

B Oh, Clark, you're such a boy! Superguy knows ⑭ _____ _____ _____ _____ lady. He can take one night off from fighting crime to take me to the prom. I've got my dress all picked ⑮ _____ _____ everything!

Stage 2 ドラマのシーン解説

日本語訳と、解説を参照しながら、ドラマの内容を確認しよう。そのあとで、Stage1の穴埋めに再チャレンジしてみよう。

A Lois, do you plan to ... I mean, ① **has** anyone asked you ...

ロイス、君は予定してるの…つまりさ、だれかに招待されたのかなぁ…

B Clark, ② **spit it out**, will you? Gosh!

クラーク、はっきり言って？ なによ？

* spit out「勇気を出してはっきり言う；白状する」 Gosh!「なによ！；なんなのよ！；もう！」

A Are you ③ **going to** the prom?

君はプロムに行くのかな？

* prom「(高校などで催される) 卒業前のパーティー」

B Well, of course, I am! Everybody's going! ④ **It'll be** a blast!

ええ、もちろんよ！ みんなが行くのよ！ すごく楽しいわよ！

* blast「にぎやかで楽しいひととき」

A Oh, so then, you already have a date, huh?

ああ、それじゃあ、もう相手はいるんだよね？

B Well, ⑤ **not officially**. I mean, he ⑥ **hasn't asked me** yet. ⑦ But I know he's going to ...

あー、正式ではないけど。つまり、まだ招待されてはいないの。でも、きっと彼は…

A I see. Uhm, okay. That's all I ⑧ **wanted to** know. Uh, see ya, I guess ...

わかった。えー、あのね、わかったよ。それだけが知りたかったんだ。あー、それじゃあ、またね…

B How ⑨ **about you**, Clark? Who are you taking?

あなたはどうなのよ、クラーク？ だれを連れていくの？

A I, to be honest, I haven't ⑩ **asked** anyone yet. I mean, I was going to. That is, I was planning to ask ... you.

僕はね、正直に言うと、まだだれも誘ってないんだよ。つまりね、僕は…つまりさ、僕は誘うつもりだったんだよ…君を。

* That is ...「つまり…；すなわち…」

B Oh, Clark! ⑪ **Don't** be silly! You know there's only one fella for me!

ああ、クラーク！ ふざけないでよ！ 私にはたったひとりの人しかいないって知ってるでしょ！

* fella「男性；少年」

A Superguy? You're ⑫ **waiting** for Superguy to ask you to the prom?

スーパーガイかい？ スーパーガイが君をプロムに招待してくれるのを待っているの？

B Sure I am! He's my steady, after all!

もちろんよ！ だって、彼は私の恋人なんだもの！

* after all「だって…なんだから」

A Lois, he's a superhero! I'm ⑬ **pretty** sure he has more important things to do than take a girl to the prom!

ロイス、彼はスーパーヒーローなんだよ！ きっと彼には、ひとりの女の子をプロムに連れていくのよりもっと大事な用があるよ。

B Oh, Clark, you're such a boy! Superguy knows ⑭ **how to treat a** lady. He can take one night off from fighting crime to take me to the prom. I've got my dress all picked ⑮ **out and** everything!

あのね、クラーク、あなたはホントにお子さまよね！ スーパーガイは女性の扱いを心得てるわ。彼なら、私をプロムに連れていくために、ひと晩、犯罪と闘うのを休むことだってできるわ。私はもうすっかりドレスを選んでるし、ほかのことも全部準備万端なのよ！

* pick out「選ぶ」　and everything「そのほかのなにやかや」

スーパーヒーロー・ドラマ　175

Stage 3 英文トランスクリプション

ドラマのシーン全体を英文の原稿で確認しながらCDで耳慣らししよう！ その上で、ドラマ・シーンの音声を聴きながら、まだできていない部分の穴埋めに再チャレンジしよう。

● ● ● ● ● ●

A Lois, do you plan to ... I mean, ① **has** anyone asked you ...

B Clark, ② **spit it out**, will you? Gosh!

A Are you ③ **going to** the prom?

B Well, of course, I am! Everybody's going! ④ **It'll be** a blast!

A Oh, so then, you already have a date, huh?

B Well, ⑤ **not officially**. I mean, he ⑥ **hasn't asked me** yet. ⑦ **But I** know he's going to ...

A I see. Uhm, okay. That's all I ⑧ **wanted to** know. Uh, see ya, I guess ...

B How ⑨ **about you**, Clark? Who are you taking?

A I, to be honest, I haven't ⑩ **asked** anyone yet. I mean, I was going to. That is, I was planning to ask ... you.

B Oh, Clark! ⑪ **Don't** be silly! You know there's only one fella for me!

A Superguy? You're ⑫ **waiting** for Superguy to ask you to the prom?

B Sure I am! He's my steady, after all!

A Lois, he's a superhero! I'm ⑬ **pretty** sure he has more important things to do than take a girl to the prom!

B Oh, Clark, you're such a boy! Superguy knows ⑭ **how to treat a** lady. He can take one night off from fighting crime to take me to the prom. I've got my dress all picked ⑮ **out and** everything!

Stage 4 音声変化をチェック

まとめとして、穴埋め部分の音声変化の特徴を**スロー・スピード**と**ナチュラル・スピード**で確認しよう。下記に示したカタカナ表記で音声変化を確認して、もう一度ドラマを聴き直してみよう。発音変化のルールは適宜復習しよう。

❶ has　　ハズ　　▶ ＿アズ
☞ has が弱化し [h] 音が脱落する。

❷ spit it out　　スピット・イット・アウト
　　　　▶ スピッディ [リ] ッダ [ラ] ウッ＿
☞ 3語が連結。2カ所の連結部で破裂音 [t] が弾音化する。out 末尾の [t] 音は脱落。

❸ going to　　ゴウイング・トゥー　　▶ ゴウイン＿ドゥ [ル] ー
☞ going 末尾の [g] 音が脱落。to の [t] 音が弾音化する。

❹ It'll be　　イットゥゥ・ビー　　▶ イッドゥ [ル] ゥビー
☞ it'll の [t] 音が弾音化する。

❺ not officially　　ナット・オフィシャリー　　▶ ナッド [ロ] フィシャリー
☞ 連結部で破裂音 [t] が弾音化する。

❻ hasn't asked me　　ハズント・アスクト・ミー　　▶ ハズナスッ＿ミー
☞ hasn't から [t] 音が脱落しつつ、asked に連結。asked からは [kt] 音が脱落する。

❼ But I　　バット・アイ　　▶ バッダ [ラ] イ
☞ 連結部で破裂音 [t] が弾音化する。

❽ wanted to　　ワンティッド・トゥー　　▶ ワニッ＿トゥー
☞ wanted から破裂音 [t] や [d] が脱落する。

❾ about you　　アバウト・ユー　　▶ アバウチュー
☞ [t] + [j] の部分で音が混じり合い、[チュ] に近い音に変化する。

❿ asked　　アスクト　　▶ アスッ＿ト
☞ asked からは [k] 音が脱落する。

⓫ Don't　　ドウント　　▶ ドン＿
☞ 弱化した Don't 末尾の [t] 音が脱落する。

⓬ waiting　　ウェイティング　　▶ ウェイディ [リ] ン＿
☞ 破裂音 [t] が弾音化する。末尾の [g] 音も脱落しやすい。

⓭ pretty　　プリティー　　▶ プリディ [リ] ー
☞ 破裂音 [t] が弾音化する。

⓮ how to treat a　　ハウ・トゥー・トゥリート・ア　▶ ハウドゥ [ル] ートリーダ [ラ]
☞ to の [t] 音や treat a の連結部の [t] 音が弾音化する。

⓯ out and　　アウト・エンド　　▶ アウデ [レ] ン＿
☞ 連結部で破裂音 [t] が弾音化する。and 末尾の [d] 音も脱落。

スーパーヒーロー・ドラマ

Unit 29 企業コメディー
Corporate Comedy (The Office type)

Stage 1 穴埋めドラマ・リスニング

音声変化に注意してCDでドラマの音声を聴きながら空欄部分を埋めてみよう。CDのナチュラル音声での聴き取りが難しいときは、次のトラックに収録されたスロー音声で聴いてみよう。

● ● ● ● ●

A Well, good morning, Dwayne. So ① _____ _____ could make it. Thank you for taking the time to ② _____ _____ _____ us.

B Aw, Nigel, ③ _____ _____ so lame. You ④ _____ _____ _____ ⑤ _____ _____ homeroom teacher.

A Oh, okay, then let's ⑥ _____ something else. The next time you come in two hours late I fire your ass!

B Still major lame-o. You can't fire me for being late after I was here till midnight last night fixing YOUR mistakes.

A First of all, they weren't my mistakes. Technically. ⑦ _____ _____, even when you've ⑧ _____ _____ excuse, you STILL have to call in when you're ⑨ _____ _____ be late.

B Nigel, ⑩ _____ _____ some slack. First, the report you screwed up so badly has now been sent out. Your ass is saved. Second, no, I do ⑪ _____ _____ you ⑫ _____ thank me. Third, I am really tired. I think I will take a nap now. Please try to avoid any major screw ups for at least the next two hours.

Ⓐ You had ⑬ _____ ⑭ _____ _____ attitude, pronto! Either start showing me more respect, or start looking for a new job! ⑮ _____ _____?

Ⓑ Huh? Sorry, no, I missed it.

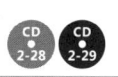

Stage 2 ドラマのシーン解説

日本語訳と、解説を参照しながら、ドラマの内容を確認しよう。そのあとで、Stage1の穴埋めに再チャレンジしてみよう。

Ⓐ Well, good morning, Dwayne. So ① **glad you** could make it. Thank you for taking the time to ② **drop in on** us.

ああ、おはよう、ドゥエイン。君にお越しいただいて非常にうれしいよ。時間を割いて弊社にお立ち寄りいただき感謝するよ。

* drop in on ...「…のところに立ち寄る」

Ⓑ Aw, Nigel, ③ **that is** so lame. You ④ **sound like a** ⑤ **second grade** homeroom teacher.

あー、ナイジェル、そりゃあまりにつまらないよ。2年生の担任みたいだ。

* Aw.「あー；バカな」反抗・失望などを表す。　lame「つまらない；独創性のない；ダサい」
  sound like ...「…のように響く；聞こえる」

企業コメディー　179

A Oh, okay, then let's ⑥ **try** something else. The next time you come in two hours late I fire your ass!

ああ、わかった。じゃあ、ほかのを試そう。今度2時間遅刻したら、お前のケツをクビにしてやる！

＊ fire「クビにする」

B Still major lame-o. You can't fire me for being late after I was here till midnight last night fixing YOUR mistakes.

まだかなりダサいな。君は僕をクビにはできないよ。昨夜、深夜まで君のミスの尻ぬぐいでここにいて遅刻したんだからさ。

＊ major「すごく；大いに」 lame-o「ダサい」 fix「ゴタゴタを解決する；始末する；修復する」

A First of all, they weren't my mistakes. Technically. ⑦ **And second**, even when you've ⑧ **got an** excuse, you STILL have to call in when you're ⑨ **going to** be late.

まず第一に、あれは私のミスじゃない。厳密にはな。で、第二に、理由があるとしても、それでも遅れるときには電話を入れてこなきゃダメなんだよ。

＊ technically「厳密には」 excuse「理由；言い訳；弁明」 call in「電話を入れる」

B Nigel, ⑩ **cut me** some slack. First, the report you screwed up so badly has now been sent out. Your ass is saved. Second, no, I do ⑪ **not expect** you ⑫ **to** thank me. Third, I am really tired. I think I will take a nap now. Please try to avoid any major screw ups for at least the next two hours.

ナイジェル、勘弁してくれよ。まず第一に、君が台無しにした報告書はもう送信済みだ。君のケツは救われたんだよ。第二に、俺は、君からの感謝なんてまったく求めていない。第三に、俺はひどく疲れてる。いまから昼寝をするよ。大きなヘマをやらかさないようにしてくださいよ。少なくとも今後2時間はさ。

＊ cut ... some slack「…を大目にみる」 screw up「台無しにする」 badly「ひどく」
　be saved「救われる」 expect A to B「AにBするように期待する」 nap「昼寝；うたた寝」

avoid「避ける」 major「大きな；目立った」

A You had ⑬ **better** ⑭ **adjust your** attitude, pronto! Either start showing me more respect, or start looking for a new job! ⑮ **Got that**?

お前は態度を改めたほうがいいな、即刻だ！ もっと私に敬意を表するか、あるいは新しい職を探すかのどっちかだ！ わかったか？

* adjust one's attitude「態度を改める」 pronto「即座に」 Either A or B.「A か B のどちらか」 respect「敬意；尊敬」

B Huh? Sorry, no, I missed it.

はぁ？ ごめん、いや、聞こえなかったよ。

* miss「逃す；聞き逃す；理解しそこなう」

Stage 3 英文トランスクリプション

ドラマのシーン全体を英文の原稿で確認しながらCDで耳慣らししよう！ その上で、ドラマ・シーンの音声を聴きながら、まだできていない部分の穴埋めに再チャレンジしよう。

● ● ● ● ● ●

A Well, good morning, Dwayne. So ① **glad you** could make it. Thank you for taking the time to ② **drop in on** us.

B Aw, Nigel, ③ **that is** so lame. You ④ **sound like a** ⑤ **second grade** homeroom teacher.

A Oh, okay, then let's ⑥ **try** something else. The next time you come in two hours late I fire your ass!

B Still major lame-o. You can't fire me for being late after I was here till midnight last night fixing YOUR mistakes.

A First of all, they weren't my mistakes. Technically. ⑦ **And second**, even when you've ⑧ **got an** excuse, you STILL have to call in when you're ⑨ **going to** be late.

B Nigel, ⑩ **cut me** some slack. First, the report you screwed up so badly has now been sent out. Your ass is saved. Second, no, I do ⑪ **not expect** you ⑫ **to** thank me. Third, I am really tired. I think I will take a nap now. Please try to avoid any major screw ups for at least the next two hours.

A You had ⑬ **better** ⑭ **adjust your** attitude, pronto! Either start showing me more respect, or start looking for a new job! ⑮ **Got that**?

B Huh? Sorry, no, I missed it.

182

Stage 4 音声変化をチェック

まとめとして、穴埋め部分の音声変化の特徴を**スロー・スピード**と**ナチュラル・スピード**で確認しよう。下記に示したカタカナ表記で音声変化を確認して、もう一度ドラマを聴き直してみよう。発音変化のルールは適宜復習しよう。

❶ **glad you** 　　　　　　グラッド・ユー　　▶ グラッジュー
  ☞ [d] + [j] の部分で音が混じり合い、[ジュ] に近い音に変化する。

❷ **drop in on** 　　　　　ドゥラップ・イン・オン　　▶ ドゥラッピノン
  ☞ 3語が連結する。

❸ **that is** 　　　　　　　ザット・イズ　　▶ ザッディ [リ] ズ
  ☞ 連結部で [t] 音が弾音化する。

❹ **sound like a** 　　　　サウンド・ライク・ア　　▶ サウン_ライカ
  ☞ sound 末尾の破裂音 [d] が脱落。like a は連結する。

❺ **second grade** 　　　　セカンド・グレイド　　▶ セカン_グレイド
  ☞ second 末尾の破裂音 [d] が脱落する。

❻ **try** 　　　　　　　　　トゥライ　　▶ チュライ
  ☞ [tr] の [t] 音は [チュ] のように変化する。

❼ **And second** 　　　　　アンド・セカンド　　▶ アン_セカン_
  ☞ 2語それぞれの末尾で破裂音 [d] が脱落する。

❽ **got an** 　　　　　　　ガット・アン　　▶ ガッダ [ラ] ン
  ☞ 連結部で [t] 音が弾音化する。

❾ **going to** 　　　　　　ゴウイング・トゥー　　▶ ゴウイン_ドゥ [ル]
  ☞ going 末尾の破裂音 [g] が脱落する。弱化した to の破裂音 [t] が弾音化する。

❿ **cut me** 　　　　　　　カット・ミー　　▶ カッ_ミー
  ☞ cut 末尾の破裂音 [t] が脱落する。

⓫ **not expect** 　　　　　ナット・エクスペクト　　▶ ナッデ [レ] クスペクト
  ☞ 連結部で [t] 音が弾音化する。

⓬ **to** 　　　　　　　　　トゥー　　▶ ドゥ [ル] ー
  ☞ 破裂音 [t] が弾音化する。

⓭ **better** 　　　　　　　ベター　　▶ ベダ [ラ] ー
  ☞ 破裂音 [t] が弾音化する。

⓮ **adjust your** 　　　　アジャスト・ユア　　▶ アジャスチュア
  ☞ [t] + [j] の部分で音が混じり合い、[チュ] に近い音に変化する。

⓯ **Got that** 　　　　　　ゴット・ザット　　▶ ゴッ_ザッ_
  ☞ 2語それぞれの末尾で破裂音 [t] が脱落する。

Unit 30 独身男性コメディー

Bachelor Comedy (Two and a Half Men type)

Stage 1 穴埋めドラマ・リスニング

音声変化に注意してCDでドラマの音声を聴きながら空欄部分を埋めてみよう。CDのナチュラル音声での聴き取りが難しいときは、次のトラックに収録されたスロー音声で聴いてみよう。

● ● ● ● ●

A So let me ① _____ _____ straight. You, my brother, are ② _____ Candy, my ex.

B Yep, ③ _____ _____ _____ the situation, yessir ... She says hi, by the way.

A But seeing as how you are now staying here at my place, can you not see how that might ④ _____ _____, complicate things?

B Yeah, I have ⑤ _____ _____ _____. And if you're ⑥ _____ _____ sometimes I plan to bring her over here, well, yes. I do.

A I've seen some really weird things in my life. But the ⑦ _____ _____ you, making ⑧ _____ _____ MY ex, on MY couch, is just a tad above my threshold.

B Chill, bro. ⑨ _____ _____ you who dumped Candy, right? On her birthday? In ⑩ _____ _____ all her friends and relatives? With her cousin ⑪ _____ _____ your lap?

184

A Yess ... ⑫ _____ _____ point is?

B Look, Candy is over you. You're over Candy. Me? I'm ⑬ _____ _____ heals over Candy. For once in my miserable, practically celibate, life, I've ⑭ _____ _____ babe girlfriend who digs me. Can't you just let me enjoy it?

A Ah, so this is jealousy, huh? You're trying to ⑮ _____ _____ _____ my face because I've always had better luck with girls than you. I see.

Stage 2 ドラマのシーン解説

日本語訳と、解説を参照しながら、ドラマの内容を確認しよう。そのあとで、Stage1の穴埋めに再チャレンジしてみよう。

A So let me ① **get this** straight. You, my brother, are ② **dating** Candy, my ex.

で、これだけははっきりさせとこうか。俺の弟のお前は、俺の元カノのキャンディーとつき合ってるんだよな。

* ex = ex-girlfriend「元カノ；別れたガールフレンド」

B Yep, ③ **that would be** the situation, yessir ... She says hi, by the way.

ああ、そういう状況だろうね、確かに…そうだ、彼女がよろしくって言ってたよ。

* situation「状況」 yessir「確かに；そのとおり」

独身男性コメディー 185

A But seeing as how you are now staying here at my place, can you not see how that might ④ **sort of**, complicate things?

だが、お前はこの俺のところに世話になっているってことからして、それがある意味、物事を混乱させるかもしれないってことがわからないのか？

* seeing as how …「…であることからして；…であるからには」
  complicate「複雑にする；困難にする」

B Yeah, I have ⑤ **thought about that**. And if you're ⑥ **wondering if** sometimes I plan to bring her over here, well, yes. I do.

ああ、それは考えたことがあるよ。それとね、たまに僕が彼女をここに連れてこようと予定してるのかどうかと思ってるのなら、ああ、そうするつもりだよ。

* wonder「…だろうかと思う」

A I've seen some really weird things in my life. But the ⑦ **thought of** you, making ⑧ **out with** MY ex, on MY couch, is just a tad above my threshold.

俺は、人生でかなり奇妙なことを見てきたよ。でも、お前が、俺のカウチの上で、俺の元カノといちゃついていると考えるのは、ちょっと俺の臨界点を超えちゃってるんだよ。

* weird「奇妙な；変わった；気味の悪い」　make out「いちゃつく；セックスする」
  threshold「境界点；域」

B Chill, bro. ⑨ **It was** you who dumped Candy, right? On her birthday? In ⑩ **front of** all her friends and relatives? With her cousin ⑪ **sitting on** your lap?

落ち着いてよ、兄貴。キャンディーを振ったのは兄貴だよね？　彼女の誕生日にね？　友達や親戚みんなの目の前でさ？　キャンディーのいとこを膝に乗っけながらね？

* dump「振る；無責任に放り出す」

A Yess … ⑫ **and your** point is?

そうさなぁ…でなにが言いたいんだよ。

* Yess ... = Yes ...

Ⓑ Look, Candy is over you. You're over Candy. Me? I'm ⑬ **head over** heals over Candy. For once in my miserable, practically celibate, life, I've ⑭ **got a** babe girlfriend who digs me. Can't you just let me enjoy it?

あのね、キャンディーはもう兄貴のことは忘れてるんだ。兄貴もキャンディーには興味ないよね。僕のほうはさ。キャンディーにぞっこんなんだよ。僕の惨めで、ほとんど独り身だった人生の中でたったの一度、僕を気に入ってくれる愛しい彼女ができたんだよ。単純にそれを楽しませてもらえないかな？

* over ...「…を忘れる；…に興味がなくなる」 be head over heals over ...「…にぞっこんだ」
  for once in one's life「人生でたった一度」 practically「実際；事実上；ほとんど」
  celibate「禁欲的な」 dig「好む；気に入る」

Ⓐ Ah, so this is jealousy, huh? You're trying to ⑮ **rub it in** my face because I've always had better luck with girls than you. I see.

ああ、じゃあ、これは嫉妬なんだな？ 俺がずっと、お前よりも女の子運に恵まれてきたからって、俺の傷口にしつこく塩を塗ろうとしてるんだな。わかったよ。

* rub it in someone's face「しつこく…の傷口に塩を塗る」
  have better luck with A than B「A に関して B よりも運がいい」

Stage 3　英文トランスクリプション

ドラマのシーン全体を英文の原稿で確認しながらCDで耳慣らしししよう！　その上で、ドラマ・シーンの音声を聴きながら、まだできていない部分の穴埋めに再チャレンジしよう。

● ● ● ● ● ●

A So let me ① **get this** straight. You, my brother, are ② **dating** Candy, my ex.

B Yep, ③ **that would be** the situation, yessir ... She says hi, by the way.

A But seeing as how you are now staying here at my place, can you not see how that might ④ **sort of**, complicate things?

B Yeah, I have ⑤ **thought about that**. And if you're ⑥ **wondering if** sometimes I plan to bring her over here, well, yes. I do.

A I've seen some really weird things in my life. But the ⑦ **thought of** you, making ⑧ **out with** MY ex, on MY couch, is just a tad above my threshold.

B Chill, bro. ⑨ **It was** you who dumped Candy, right? On her birthday? In ⑩ **front of** all her friends and relatives? With her cousin ⑪ **sitting on** your lap?

A Yess ... ⑫ **and your** point is?

B Look, Candy is over you. You're over Candy. Me? I'm ⑬ **head over** heals over Candy. For once in my miserable, practically celibate, life, I've ⑭ **got a** babe girlfriend who digs me. Can't you just let me enjoy it?

A Ah, so this is jealousy, huh? You're trying to ⑮ **rub it in** my face because I've always had better luck with girls than you. I see.

Stage 4　音声変化をチェック

まとめとして、穴埋め部分の音声変化の特徴を**スロー・スピード**と**ナチュラル・スピード**で確認しよう。下記に示したカタカナ表記で音声変化を確認して、もう一度ドラマを聴き直してみよう。発音変化のルールは適宜復習しよう。

❶ get this　　　　　　　　　ゲット・ズィス　　　　　▶ ゲッ＿ズィス
☞ get の破裂音 [t] が脱落する。

❷ dating　　　　　　　　　　デイティング　　　　　　▶ デイディ [リ] ン＿
☞ 破裂音 [t] が弾音化する。末尾の [g] 音も脱落する。

❸ that would be　　　　　　ザット・ウッド・ビー　　　▶ ザッ＿ウッ＿ビー
☞ that と would 末尾の破裂音が脱落する。

❹ sort of　　　　　　　　　　ソート・アヴ　　　　　　▶ ソーダ [ラ] ヴ
☞ 連結部で [t] 音が弾音化する。

❺ thought about that　　　　ソート・アバウト・ザット　▶ ソーダ [ラ] バウッ＿ザッ＿
☞ thought about の連結部で [t] 音が弾音化する。about や that 末尾の破裂音 [t] が脱落する。

❻ wondering if　　　　　　　ワンダリング・イフ　　　　▶ ワンダリニフ
☞ wondering 末尾の破裂音 [g] が脱落しつつ、if と連結する。

❼ thought of　　　　　　　　ソート・アヴ　　　　　　▶ ソーダ [ラ] ヴ
☞ 連結部で [t] 音が弾音化する。

❽ out with　　　　　　　　　アウト・ウィズ　　　　　　▶ アウッ＿ウィズ
☞ out 末尾の破裂音 [t] が脱落する。

❾ It was　　　　　　　　　　イット・ワズ　　　　　　　▶ イッ＿ワズ
☞ it 末尾の破裂音 [t] が脱落する。

❿ front of　　　　　　　　　フラント・アヴ　　　　　　▶ フラナヴ
☞ front 末尾の破裂音 [t] が脱落しつつ、of と連結する。

⓫ sitting on　　　　　　　　スィッティング・オン　　　▶ スィッディ [リ] ノン
☞ sitting の破裂音 [t] が弾音化する。sitting 末尾の破裂音 [g] が脱落しつつ、on と連結する。

⓬ and your　　　　　　　　　アンド・ユア　　　　　　　▶ アンジュア
☞ [d] + [j] の部分で音が混じり合い、[ジュ] に近い音に変化する。

⓭ head over　　　　　　　　ヘッド・オウヴァー　　　　▶ ヘッド [ロ] ウヴァー
☞ 連結部で [d] 音が弾音化する。

⓮ got a　　　　　　　　　　　ガット・ア　　　　　　　　▶ ガッダ [ラ]
☞ 連結部で [t] 音が弾音化する。

⓯ rub it in　　　　　　　　　ラブ・イット・イン　　　　▶ ラビッディ [リ] ン
☞ 3語が連結。it in の連結部で破裂音 [t] が弾音化する。

独身男性コメディー　189

Unit 31 スポーツ・コメディー

Sports Comedy (Anger Management type)

Stage 1 穴埋めドラマ・リスニング

音声変化に注意してCDでドラマの音声を聴きながら空欄部分を埋めてみよう。CDのナチュラル音声での聴き取りが難しいときは、次のトラックに収録されたスロー音声で聴いてみよう。

● ● ● ● ●

A So you were a pro athlete, huh? That's so awesome! How many touchdowns ① _____ _____, uh ... make?

B Ah, a sports fan, I see. Touchdowns are for football. I played baseball. For the Dodgers. You've ② _____ _____ them?

A Of COURSE! Wow, you were a Dodger? That's ③ _____ cool! Tell me ④ _____ _____ career!

B Well, I don't like to brag. But I DID win the Gold Glove three straight years, back ⑤ _____ _____ late ⑥ _____ ...

A The Gold Glove! So you were a boxer too? So, like, multi-talented!

B The Gold Glove is a BASEBALL award. For fielding. See, every year, they ... you, uh, ⑦ _____ _____ a thing about sports, do you?

A Oops! You ⑧ _____ _____! ⑨ _____ _____ my pants down!

190

B Ahem ... !!! Um, hopefully we'll ⑩ _____ _____ that
⑪ _____.

A ⑫ _____ _____ DO know about sports is that pro athletes are successful, and confident. And ⑬ _____ _____ fit, hard, sexy bodies!

B Say, you wanna ⑭ _____ _____ _____ here? We could take a drive along the coast.

A I've ⑮ _____ _____ _____ idea. We go back to your place. And when we get there, I'll teach you how to play MY favorite sport.

Stage 2 ドラマのシーン解説

日本語訳と、解説を参照しながら、ドラマの内容を確認しよう。そのあとで、Stage1の穴埋めに再チャレンジしてみよう。

A So you were a pro athlete, huh? That's so awesome! How many touchdowns ① **did you**, uh ... make?

で、あなたはプロのアスリートだったの？ すごいわ！ 何回タッチダウン…うーん、したの？

∗ awesome「すごい；かっこいい」

B Ah, a sports fan, I see. Touchdowns are for football. I played baseball. For the Dodgers. You've ② **heard of** them?

ああ、スポーツ・ファンねぇ、そうか〜。タッチダウンはアメフトで、僕は野球をやってたんだよね。ドジャーズにいたんだ。聞いたことはあるかなぁ？

スポーツ・コメディー 191

Ⓐ Of COURSE! Wow, you were a Dodger? That's ③ **totally** cool! Tell me ④ **about your** career!

もちろんよ！ へ〜、ドジャーズの選手だったの？ 超カッコいい！ あなたの選手人生を教えてよ！

* totally「まったく；完全に」

Ⓑ Well, I don't like to brag. But I DID win the Gold Glove three straight years, back ⑤ **in the** late ⑥ **nineties** ...

うーん、自慢じゃないけどさ、3年連続でゴールデン・グラブ賞を獲ったんだよ。90年代の終わりにさ…

* brag「自慢する」 straight「連続した」

Ⓐ The Gold Glove! So you were a boxer too? So, like, multi-talented!

ゴールデン・グラブ！ じゃあ、あなたはボクサーもやってたのね？ ものすごく、そう、マルチな才能よね！

* multi-talented「複数の才能のある；多才な」

Ⓑ The Gold Glove is a BASEBALL award. For fielding. See, every year, they ... you, uh, ⑦ **don't know** a thing about sports, do you?

ゴールデン・グラブ賞は野球の賞だよ。守備のね。あのね、毎年さ、野球ではね…君は全然スポーツのこと知らないよね、どうなの？

* fielding「(野球の) 守備」 not ... a thing「少しも…ない」

Ⓐ Oops! You ⑧ **got me**! ⑨ **Caught with** my pants down!

おっ！ そうなの〜！ 恥ずかし〜っ！

* caught with someon's pants down「…の恥ずかしいところを見つけられて」

B Ahem ... !!! Um, hopefully we'll ⑩ **get to** that ⑪ **later**.

あのさー…！　いやー、できれば、その話はあとでしよう。

A ⑫ **What I** DO know about sports is that pro athletes are successful, and confident. And ⑬ **they have** fit, hard, sexy bodies!

私が知っているのはね、プロ選手は成功していて、自信に満ちているの。で、すごく頑強でセクシーなカラダをしてるのよ！

....

＊ fit「壮健な；元気な」

B Say, you wanna ⑭ **get out of** here? We could take a drive along the coast.

例えばさ、ここを出たいとか思う？　海岸沿いをドライブしてもいいよ。

....

＊ get out of ...「…を出る；抜け出す」　coast「海岸；沿岸」

A I've ⑮ **got a better** idea. We go back to your place. And when we get there, I'll teach you how to play MY favorite sport.

私にはもっといいアイデアがあるわ。あなたの家に戻りましょう。で、到着したら、私の好みのスポーツをやり方を、私があなたに教えてあげるの。

Stage 3 英文トランスクリプション

ドラマのシーン全体を英文の原稿で確認しながらCDで耳慣らししよう！ その上で、ドラマ・シーンの音声を聴きながら、まだできていない部分の穴埋めに再チャレンジしよう。

● ● ● ● ● ●

A So you were a pro athlete, huh? That's so awesome! How many touchdowns ① **did you**, uh … make?

B Ah, a sports fan, I see. Touchdowns are for football. I played baseball. For the Dodgers. You've ② **heard of** them?

A Of COURSE! Wow, you were a Dodger? That's ③ **totally** cool! Tell me ④ **about your** career!

B Well, I don't like to brag. But I DID win the Gold Glove three straight years, back ⑤ **in the** late ⑥ **nineties** …

A The Gold Glove! So you were a boxer too? So, like, multi-talented!

B The Gold Glove is a BASEBALL award. For fielding. See, every year, they … you, uh, ⑦ **don't know** a thing about sports, do you?

A Oops! You ⑧ **got me!** ⑨ **Caught with** my pants down!

B Ahem … !!! Um, hopefully we'll ⑩ **get to** that ⑪ **later**.

A ⑫ **What I** DO know about sports is that pro athletes are successful, and confident. And ⑬ **they have** fit, hard, sexy bodies!

B Say, you wanna ⑭ **get out of** here? We could take a drive along the coast.

A I've ⑮ **got a better** idea. We go back to your place. And when we get there, I'll teach you how to play MY favorite sport.

Stage 4 音声変化をチェック

まとめとして、穴埋め部分の音声変化の特徴を**スロー・スピード**と**ナチュラル・スピード**で確認しよう。下記に示したカタカナ表記で音声変化を確認して、もう一度ドラマを聴き直してみよう。発音変化のルールは適宜復習しよう。

❶ did you ディッド・ユー ▶ ディッジュー
☞ [d]＋[j] の部分で音が混じり合い、[ジュ] に近い音に変化する。

❷ heard of ハード・アヴ ▶ ハーダ [ラ] (ヴ)
☞ 連結部の破裂音 [d] が弾音化する。

❸ totally トウタリー ▶ トウダ [ラ] リー
☞ 中程の破裂音 [t] が弾音化する。

❹ about your アバウト・ユア ▶ アバウッ＿ユア
☞ about の破裂音 [t] が脱落する。

❺ in the イン・ザ ▶ イナ
☞ [n]＋[ð] が [n] 音に変化する。

❻ nineties ナインティーズ ▶ ナインディ [リ] ーズ
☞ 破裂音 [t] が弾音化する。

❼ don't know ドゥント・ノウ ▶ ドノウ
☞ 弱化した don't から [t] 音が脱落しつつ、know に連結する。

❽ got me ガット・ミー ▶ ガッ＿ミー
☞ got の破裂音 [t] が脱落する。

❾ Caught with コート・ウィズ ▶ コーッ＿ウィズ
☞ Caught の破裂音 [t] が脱落する。

❿ get to ゲット・トゥー ▶ ゲッ＿トゥー
☞ get の破裂音 [t] が脱落する。

⓫ later レイター ▶ レイダ [ラ] ー
☞ 破裂音 [t] が弾音化する。

⓬ What I ワット・アイ ▶ ワッダ [ラ] イ
☞ 連結部で破裂音 [t] が弾音化する。

⓭ they have ゼイ・ハヴ ▶ ゼイ＿アヴ
☞ have が弱化して [əv] と発音される。

⓮ get out of ゲット・アウト・アヴ ▶ ゲッダ [ラ] ウダ [ラ] ヴ
☞ 3語が連結。2カ所の連結部で破裂音 [t] が弾音化する。

⓯ got a better ガット・ア・ベター ▶ ガッダ [ラ] ベダ [ラ] ー
☞ got a の連結部や better で破裂音 [t] が弾音化する。

Unit 32 バー・コメディー
Bar Comedy (Cheers type)

Stage 1 穴埋めドラマ・リスニング

音声変化に注意してCDでドラマの音声を聴きながら空欄部分を埋めてみよう。CDのナチュラル音声での聴き取りが難しいときは、次のトラックに収録されたスロー音声で聴いてみよう。

● ● ● ● ●

A Life can be ① _____ weird, huh? I mean, who ② _____ _____ guessed that we would end up together?

B I know! We are probably the LAST two people anyone ③ _____ _____ imagined as a couple.

A I ④ _____ stand you that first night! You were so stuck-up. You acted like you were the only one in the bar ⑤ _____ _____ ever ⑥ _____ _____ novel.

B Stan, I WAS the only person in the bar who had ever read a novel.

A Okay, I'll give you that. ⑦ _____ _____ me? I must have seemed a ⑧ _____ cocky, huh?

B Cocky? You were obnoxious! It was clear you thought you ⑨ _____ _____ _____ woman you ⑩ _____ _____ sleep with you.

A Uh huh? And was I wrong? I mean, considering …

B Oh, please! That first night, if ⑪ _____ _____ ⑫ _____ _____ ⑬ _____ _____ me I would have laughed in your face!

A Deeane, believe me, that first night, ⑭ _____ on you was the furthest thing from my mind.

B Is that so? So, let's see ... you DIDN'T offer me a job that night ⑮ _____ _____ you could have an excuse to see more of me? Just being a good Samaritan, huh?

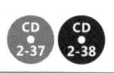

Stage 2　ドラマのシーン解説

日本語訳と、解説を参照しながら、ドラマの内容を確認しよう。そのあとで、Stage1の穴埋めに再チャレンジしてみよう。

A Life can be ① **pretty** weird, huh? I mean, who ② **would have** guessed that we would end up together?

人生って奇妙なものだよね？ つまりさ、僕らがいっしょになるって、だれが想像しただろうね？

＊ weird「奇妙な」　end up ...「結局…になる」

B I know! We are probably the LAST two people anyone ③ **could have** imagined as a couple.

そうよね！ 私たちって、だれかがカップルだって想像できた最後のふたりよね。

＊ imagine「想像する」

バー・コメディー　197

A I ④ **couldn't** stand you that first night! You were so stuck-up. You acted like you were the only one in the bar ⑤ **who had** ever ⑥ **read a** novel.

僕は最初の夜、君のことが我慢できなかったんだよ！ 君はものすごくお高くとまっていたよね。バーの中では、小説を読んだことのあるたったひとりの人間みたいに振る舞ってたよ。

* stuck-up「お高くとまって」

B Stan, I WAS the only person in the bar who had ever read a novel.

スタン、私は、バーで小説を読んだことがある唯一の人間だったわ。

A Okay, I'll give you that. ⑦ **What about** me? I must have seemed a ⑧ **little** cocky, huh?

わかったよ。その点は譲るから。僕に関してはどう？ ちょっとうぬぼれて見えたんだろうね？

* cocky「生意気な；うぬぼれた」

B Cocky? You were obnoxious! It was clear you thought you ⑨ **could get any** woman you ⑩ **wanted to** sleep with you.

うぬぼれてる？ あなたは不愉快だったわよ！ あなたは、寝たいと思った女は全部手に入るだろうと思ってるのがよくわかったから。

* obnoxious「不愉快な」

A Uh huh? And was I wrong? I mean, considering …

へえ。で、僕は間違ってたかな？ つまりね、考えるとさ、ほら…

B Oh, please! That first night, if ⑪ **you had** ⑫ **tried to** ⑬ **hit on** me I would have laughed in your face!

ああ、冗談じゃないわ！ あの最初の夜、あなたが私に言い寄ろうとしていたら、面と向かってあざ笑ってやってたわよ。

＊ laugh in someone's face「面と向かってあざ笑う」

Ⓐ Deeane, believe me, that first night, ⑭ **hitting** on you was the furthest thing from my mind.

ディアンヌ〜、信じてくれよ、あの最初の夜、君に言い寄るなんて僕の頭の中じゃいちばんあり得ないことだったんだから。

＊ furthest「もっとも遠く離れて」

Ⓑ Is that so? So, let's see … you DIDN'T offer me a job that night ⑮ **so that** you could have an excuse to see more of me? Just being a good Samaritan, huh?

そうなの？ で、そうね…あなたはあの夜、もっと頻繁に私に会う口実を作るために私に仕事をくれたんじゃなかったの？ 情け深い善良な市民を演じながら、ね？

＊ excuse「口実」　see more of someone = see someone more often
　good Samaritan「善良な市民；慈悲深い人」

Stage 3 英文トランスクリプション

ドラマのシーン全体を英文の原稿で確認しながらCDで耳慣らししよう！ その上で、ドラマ・シーンの音声を聴きながら、まだできていない部分の穴埋めに再チャレンジしよう。

● ● ● ● ● ●

A Life can be ① **pretty** weird, huh? I mean, who ② **would have** guessed that we would end up together?

B I know! We are probably the LAST two people anyone ③ **could have** imagined as a couple.

A I ④ **couldn't** stand you that first night! You were so stuck-up. You acted like you were the only one in the bar ⑤ **who had** ever ⑥ **read a** novel.

B Stan, I WAS the only person in the bar who had ever read a novel.

A Okay, I'll give you that. ⑦ **What about** me? I must have seemed a ⑧ **little** cocky, huh?

B Cocky? You were obnoxious! It was clear you thought you ⑨ **could get any** woman you ⑩ **wanted to** sleep with you.

A Uh huh? And was I wrong? I mean, considering …

B Oh, please! That first night, if ⑪ **you had** ⑫ **tried to** ⑬ **hit on** me I would have laughed in your face!

A Deeane, believe me, that first night, ⑭ **hitting** on you was the furthest thing from my mind.

B Is that so? So, let's see … you DIDN'T offer me a job that night ⑮ **so that** you could have an excuse to see more of me? Just being a good Samaritan, huh?

Stage 4 音声変化をチェック

まとめとして、穴埋め部分の音声変化の特徴を**スロー・スピード**と**ナチュラル・スピード**で確認しよう。下記に示したカタカナ表記で音声変化を確認して、もう一度ドラマを聴き直してみよう。発音変化のルールは適宜復習しよう。

❶ pretty 　　　　　　　プリティー　　　　　　▶ プリディ [リ] ー
　☞ 破裂音 [t] が弾音化する。

❷ would have 　　　　ウッド・ハヴ　　　　　　▶ ウッダヴ
　☞ would が弱化した have [əv] に連結する。

❸ could have 　　　　クッド・ハヴ　　　　　　▶ クッダヴ
　☞ could が弱化した have [əv] に連結する。

❹ couldn't 　　　　　クドゥント　　　　　　　▶ クドゥン＿
　☞ 末尾の破裂音 [t] が脱落する。

❺ who had 　　　　　　フー・ハッド　　　　　　▶ フー＿アド
　☞ had が弱化して [əv] と発音される。

❻ read a 　　　　　　レッド・ア　　　　　　　▶ レッダ
　☞ 2語が連結する。

❼ What about 　　　　ワット・アバウト　　　　▶ ワッダ [ラ] バウッ＿
　☞ 連結部で [t] 音が弾音化する。about 末尾の [t] 音が脱落する。

❽ little 　　　　　　リトゥゥ　　　　　　　　▶ リドゥ [ル] ゥ
　☞ 破裂音 [t] が弾音化する。

❾ could get any 　　クッド・ゲット・エニィ　▶ クッ＿ゲッデ [レ] ニィ
　☞ could の破裂音 [d] が脱落。get any の連結部で [t] 音が弾音化する。

❿ wanted to 　　　　ワンティッド・トゥー　　▶ ワニッ＿ドゥ [ル] ー
　☞ wanted から [t] 音や [d] 音が脱落。to の破裂音 [t] が弾音化する。

⓫ you had 　　　　　ユー・ハッド　　　　　　▶ ユー＿ッド
　☞ had が弱化し [d] の音だけになる。

⓬ tried to 　　　　トゥライド・トゥー　　　▶ トゥライ＿ドゥ [ル] ー
　☞ tried から [d] 音が脱落。to の破裂音 [t] が弾音化する。

⓭ hit on 　　　　　ヒット・オン　　　　　　▶ ヒッド [ロ] ン
　☞ 連結部で [t] 音が弾音化する。

⓮ hitting 　　　　　ヒッティング　　　　　　▶ ヒッディ [リ] ン＿
　☞ 破裂音 [t] が弾音化する。末尾の [g] 音が脱落する。

⓯ so that 　　　　　ソウ・ザット　　　　　　▶ ソザッ＿
　☞ so は弱化して [sə] のみの発音になる。that 末尾の破裂音 [t] が脱落する。

Unit 33 犯罪捜査ドラマ
Crime Investigation Drama (CSI type)

Stage 1 穴埋めドラマ・リスニング

音声変化に注意してCDでドラマの音声を聴きながら空欄部分を埋めてみよう。CDのナチュラル音声での聴き取りが難しいときは、次のトラックに収録されたスロー音声で聴いてみよう。

● ● ● ● ● ●

A So ① _____ _____ we got?

B Well, we don't have much, that's for sure. Whoever did this was very thorough ② _____ covering up his tracks.

A So, ③ _____ _____ premeditated?

B ④ _____ _____, _____ can't say. Somehow, my gut tells me no. We have someone here who was very violent, most likely ⑤ _____ _____ _____ _____ rage.
⑥ _____ _____ very smart, and very determined not to get caught.

A So, no fingerprints? No hairs? Blood? Nothing we can get DNA samples from?

B ⑦ _____ _____ thing. It's like a ghost walked in here ⑧ _____ chopped this guy to pieces.

A The victim's wife is ⑨ _____ _____ way over. There's uh, no reason for her to see this, is there?

B No, keep her outside. You ⑩ _____ _____ was the maid who called this in, right? Was that her that was ⑪ _____ on the stairs ⑫ _____ _____ _____ here?

A Yeah, she was really shook-up. I think she's calm enough to talk now. You ⑬ _____ _____ word with her?

B No, let the detective who's been assigned to this take care of that. Just keep everybody ⑭ _____ _____ here for another hour or so. There's something I ⑮ _____ figure out about this scene, something that's bothering me.

Stage 2 ドラマのシーン解説

日本語訳と、解説を参照しながら、ドラマの内容を確認しよう。そのあとで、Stage1の穴埋めに再チャレンジしてみよう。

A So ① **what have** we got?

で、なにかわかったことは？

B Well, we don't have much, that's for sure. Whoever did this was very thorough ② **about** covering up his tracks.

ええ、あまりよくはわからないのよ。それは確かね。だれがこれを実行したにせよ、そいつは自分の形跡を消すことを非常に徹底しているわ。

＊ whoever ...「だれが…しようとも」　thorough「徹底的な」　cover up「隠蔽する」

A So, ③ **was it** premeditated?

犯罪捜査ドラマ　203

ということは、計画的な犯行だったのだろうか？

＊ premeditated「前もって周到に計画された」

Ⓑ ④ **Even that, I** can't say. Somehow, my gut tells me no. We have someone here who was very violent, most likely ⑤ **in a fit of** rage. ⑥ **But also** very smart, and very determined not to get caught.

それさえも、はっきりとはわからないわ。なんとなく、私の本能は違うと言ってるの。ここにはだれかとても凶暴な奴がいて、おそらくはひどくカッとなっていたのでしょう。でも、同時にとても賢くて、捕まらないと強く心に決めていた。

＊ gut tells me ...「本能が私に…と教えてくれる」　in a fit of rage「カッとなって」
determined「決意して」

Ⓐ So, no fingerprints? No hairs? Blood? Nothing we can get DNA samples from?

では、指紋も残っていない？ 髪の毛も？ 血液も？ DNAサンプルが採れるものはなにもないと？

Ⓑ ⑦ **Not a** thing. It's like a ghost walked in here ⑧ **and** chopped this guy to pieces.

なにひとつ。まるで幽霊が歩いてここに入り込み、この男をバラバラに切り刻んだみたいよ。

＊ chop ... to pieces「…をバラバラに切り刻む；ぶった切る」

Ⓐ The victim's wife is ⑨ **on her** way over. There's uh, no reason for her to see this, is there?

被害者の妻がこちらに向かっているんだ。彼女にこれを見せる理由はないよね？

Ⓑ No, keep her outside. You ⑩ **said it** was the maid who called this in, right? Was that her that was ⑪ **sitting** on the stairs

⑫ **when I got** here?

ないわ。彼女は中に入れないで。この件を電話で知らせてきたのはメイドだと言ったわよね？ 私がここに到着したときに階段に座っていたのが彼女？

* keep ... outside「…を中に入れない」

Ⓐ Yeah, she was really shook-up. I think she's calm enough to talk now. You ⑬ **want a** word with her?

うん、かなりショックを受けていたよ。もう話ができるくらい落ち着いていると思う。彼女の話を聞きたいのかい？

* shook-up「気が動転して」　word「手短な会話」

Ⓑ No, let the detective who's been assigned to this take care of that. Just keep everybody ⑭ **out of** here for another hour or so. There's something I ⑮ **gotta** figure out about this scene, something that's bothering me.

いや、この件の担当刑事に任せましょう。今後、1時間ほどはだれもここに入れないで。この現場に関して、考えなきゃならないなにかがあるの。そのなにかが私を悩ませているのよ。

* assigned to ...「…を担当している」　figure out「考える；考えた末に理解する」
　bother「悩ませる」

犯罪捜査ドラマ

Stage 3 英文トランスクリプション

ドラマのシーン全体を英文の原稿で確認しながらCDで耳慣らししよう！ その上で、ドラマ・シーンの音声を聴きながら、まだできていない部分の穴埋めに再チャレンジしよう。

● ● ● ● ● ●

A So ① **what have** we got?

B Well, we don't have much, that's for sure. Whoever did this was very thorough ② **about** covering up his tracks.

A So, ③ **was it** premeditated?

B ④ **Even that, I** can't say. Somehow, my gut tells me no. We have someone here who was very violent, most likely ⑤ **in a fit of** rage. ⑥ **But also** very smart, and very determined not to get caught.

A So, no fingerprints? No hairs? Blood? Nothing we can get DNA samples from?

B ⑦ **Not a** thing. It's like a ghost walked in here ⑧ **and** chopped this guy to pieces.

A The victim's wife is ⑨ **on her** way over. There's uh, no reason for her to see this, is there?

B No, keep her outside. You ⑩ **said it** was the maid who called this in, right? Was that her that was ⑪ **sitting** on the stairs ⑫ **when I got** here?

A Yeah, she was really shook-up. I think she's calm enough to talk now. You ⑬ **want a** word with her?

B No, let the detective who's been assigned to this take care of that. Just keep everybody ⑭ **out of** here for another hour or so. There's something I ⑮ **gotta** figure out about this scene, something that's bothering me.

Stage 4 音声変化をチェック

まとめとして、穴埋め部分の音声変化の特徴を**スロー・スピード**と**ナチュラル・スピード**で確認しよう。下記に示したカタカナ表記で音声変化を確認して、もう一度ドラマを聴き直してみよう。発音変化のルールは適宜復習しよう。

❶ what have 　　　ワット・ハヴ 　　　▶ ワッダ [ラ] ヴ
☞ what が弱化した have [əv] に連結する。連結部で [t] 音が弾音化する。

❷ about 　　　アバウト 　　　▶ アバウッ＿
☞ 末尾の破裂音 [t] が脱落する。

❸ was it 　　　ワズ・イット 　　　▶ ワズィッ＿
☞ 2語が連結。it 末尾の破裂音 [t] 音が脱落する。

❹ Even that, I 　　　イーヴン・ザット・アイ 　　　▶ イーヴナッダ [ラ] イ
☞ Even that の連結部で [n] + [ð] が [n] 音に変化する。that I の連結部では、破裂音 [t] が弾音化する。

❺ in a fit of 　　　イン・ア・フィット・アヴ 　　　▶ イナフィッダ [ラ] ヴ
☞ in a は連結。fit of の連結部で破裂音 [t] が弾音化する。

❻ But also 　　　バット・オーゥソウ 　　　▶ バッド [ロ] ーゥソウ
☞ 連結部で [t] 音が弾音化する。

❼ Not a 　　　ナット・ア 　　　▶ ナッダ [ラ]
☞ 連結部で [t] 音が弾音化する。

❽ and 　　　アンド 　　　▶ アン＿
☞ 末尾の [d] 音が脱落する。

❾ on her 　　　オン・ハー 　　　▶ オナー
☞ on に弱化した her [ər] が連結する。

❿ said it 　　　セッド・イット 　　　▶ セッディッ＿
☞ 2語が連結。it の末尾の破裂音 [t] が脱落する。

⓫ sitting 　　　スィッティング 　　　▶ スィッディ [リ] ング
☞ 破裂音 [t] が弾音化する。

⓬ when I got 　　　ウェン・アイ・ガット 　　　▶ ウェナイガッ＿
☞ when I は連結。got 末尾の破裂音 [t] が脱落する。

⓭ want a 　　　ワント・ア 　　　▶ ワナ
☞ want 末尾の破裂音 [t] が脱落しつつ、a に連結する。

⓮ out of 　　　アウト・アヴ 　　　▶ アウダ [ラ] ヴ
☞ 連結部で [t] 音が弾音化する。

⓯ gotta 　　　ゴッタ 　　　▶ ゴッダ [ラ]
☞ 破裂音 [t] が弾音化する。

Unit 34 戦争ドラマ
War Drama (Band of Brothers type)

Stage 1 穴埋めドラマ・リスニング

音声変化に注意してCDでドラマの音声を聴きながら空欄部分を埋めてみよう。CDのナチュラル音声での聴き取りが難しいときは、次のトラックに収録されたスロー音声で聴いてみよう。

● ● ● ● ● ●

A Captain Daniels. Always a pleasure ① _____ see you, sir. How is Colonel Dickerson?

B ② _____ _____, Lieutenant. Please, ③ _____ _____. Colonel Dickerson conveys his personal regards to you. He continues to be impressed by the work you and your ④ _____ _____ doing.

A Thank you, sir.

B Lieutenant, I am afraid that's both good and bad news. As the most successful unit in this operating zone, we realize ⑤ _____ _____ great deal is ⑥ _____ of you.

A Yes, sir. And if I may be frank, my men are exhausted. We were hoping that you'd come to tell us we'd be ⑦ _____ some ⑧ _____ _____ _____ soon.

B I really wish that were the case. Lieutenant Jeffreys, the war is ⑨ _____ _____ _____ phase now. We've had some successes, and much of ⑩ _____ _____ due ⑪ _____ you and your men. ⑫ _____ _____ our gains are at risk now.

208

A Sir, I lost three men in just my last mission. We are being ⑬ _____.

B You'll get reinforcements. I know how close you are to all your men, and how each loss stings. ⑭ _____ _____ critical mission has come up, and the colonel has ⑮ _____ me to assign your platoon. It begins tomorrow. I'm sorry.

Stage 2 ドラマのシーン解説

日本語訳と、解説を参照しながら、ドラマの内容を確認しよう。そのあとで、Stage1の穴埋めに再チャレンジしてみよう。

A Captain Daniels. Always a pleasure ① **to** see you, sir. How is Colonel Dickerson?

ダニエルズ大尉、お会いできて光栄です。ディッカーソン大佐はいかがですか？

＊ captain「大尉」　colonel「大佐」

B ② **At ease**, Lieutenant. Please, ③ **sit down**. Colonel Dickerson conveys his personal regards to you. He continues to be impressed by the work you and your ④ **men are** doing.

中尉、気楽にして、座りなさい。ディッカーソン大佐から、君によろしく伝えてくれと言われている。大佐は、君と君の部下たちの仕事をずっと評価していらっしゃる。

戦争ドラマ　209

* lieutenant「中尉」 be impressed「感心させられる」

A Thank you, sir.

ありがとうございます。

B Lieutenant, I am afraid that's both good and bad news. As the most successful unit in this operating zone, we realize ⑤ **that a** great deal is ⑥ **asked** of you.

中尉、悪いが、大佐の君たちへの評価は、いい知らせでもあり、悪い知らせでもある。この作戦領域でもっとも成果を上げている部隊として、君たちには多くの要求があることはわかっている。

* that's both ... この that は「ディッカーソンが中尉とその部隊を評価していること」を指す。
operating zone「作戦領域」 unit「部隊」

A Yes, sir. And if I may be frank, my men are exhausted. We were hoping that you'd come to tell us we'd be ⑦ **getting** some ⑧ **r and r** soon.

はい。で、率直にお話ししてよろしければ、私の兵たちは疲れ切っております。あなたが、われわれに少々の休養と気晴らしを与えると伝えにきてくれたらと望んでおりました。

* frank「率直な」 exhausted「ひどく疲れて」
r and r = rest and recuperation「休養と気晴らし」

B I really wish that were the case. Lieutenant Jeffreys, the war is ⑨ **in a critical** phase now. We've had some successes, and much of ⑩ **that is** due ⑪ **to** you and your men. ⑫ **But all** our gains are at risk now.

そうだったら、ほんとうによいのだが。ジェフリーズ中尉、戦争はいまや重大な局面に入っている。われわれは多くの成功を収めたが、その多くは君と君の部隊の功績だ。しかし、われわれの獲得した地域が危機に瀕しているのだ。

* critical phase「重大な局面」 due to ...「…のために」 gain = gained territory in war at risk「危機に瀕して」

A Sir, I lost three men in just my last mission. We are being ⑬ **gutted**.

私はちょうどこの前のミッションで 3 名の兵を失いました。わが隊は、ガタガタなのです。

＊ gutted「ガタガタの；大打撃を受けた」

B You'll get reinforcements. I know how close you are to all your men, and how each loss stings. ⑭ **But a** critical mission has come up, and the colonel has ⑮ **instructed** me to assign your platoon. It begins tomorrow. I'm sorry.

君の部隊は補強を受ける。君が兵士たちにどれほど親密に接しているかはわかっているし、ひとつひとつの喪失がどれほどの痛みなのかもわかってはいる。しかし、重大なミッションが持ち上がり、君の小隊を割り当てるよう、大佐が私に命令を与えたのだ。ミッションは明日から開始される。申し訳ないが。

＊ reinforcement「補強；増強」　sting「傷つける；苦しませる」　critical「重大な」　platoon「小隊」

Stage 3 英文トランスクリプション

ドラマのシーン全体を英文の原稿で確認しながらCDで耳慣らししよう！ その上で、ドラマ・シーンの音声を聴きながら、まだできていない部分の穴埋めに再チャレンジしよう。

• • • • • •

A Captain Daniels. Always a pleasure ① **to** see you, sir. How is Colonel Dickerson?

B ② **At ease**, Lieutenant. Please, ③ **sit down**. Colonel Dickerson conveys his personal regards to you. He continues to be impressed by the work you and your ④ **men are** doing.

A Thank you, sir.

B Lieutenant, I am afraid that's both good and bad news. As the most successful unit in this operating zone, we realize ⑤ **that a** great deal is ⑥ **asked** of you.

A Yes, sir. And if I may be frank, my men are exhausted. We were hoping that you'd come to tell us we'd be ⑦ **getting** some ⑧ **r and r** soon.

B I really wish that were the case. Lieutenant Jeffreys, the war is ⑨ **in a critical** phase now. We've had some successes, and much of ⑩ **that is** due ⑪ **to** you and your men. ⑫ **But all** our gains are at risk now.

A Sir, I lost three men in just my last mission. We are being ⑬ **gutted**.

B You'll get reinforcements. I know how close you are to all your men, and how each loss stings. ⑭ **But a** critical mission has come up, and the colonel has ⑮ **instructed** me to assign your platoon. It begins tomorrow. I'm sorry.

Stage 4 音声変化をチェック

まとめとして、穴埋め部分の音声変化の特徴を**スロー・スピード**と**ナチュラル・スピード**で確認しよう。下記に示したカタカナ表記で音声変化を確認して、もう一度ドラマを聴き直してみよう。発音変化のルールは適宜復習しよう。

❶ to 　　　　　　　　　　　　トゥー　　　　　　　　　▶ ドゥ [ル] ー
☞ 破裂音 [t] が弾音化する。

❷ At ease 　　　　　　　　　アット・イーズ　　　　　　▶ アッディ [リ] ーズ
☞ 連結部で破裂音 [t] が弾音化する。

❸ sit down 　　　　　　　　スィット・ダウン　　　　　　▶ スィッ＿ダウン
☞ sit 末尾の破裂音 [t] 音が脱落する。

❹ men are 　　　　　　　　　メン・アー　　　　　　　　▶ メナー
☞ 2語が連結する。

❺ that a 　　　　　　　　　　ザット・ア　　　　　　　　▶ ザッダ [ラ]
☞ 連結部で破裂音 [t] が弾音化する。

❻ asked 　　　　　　　　　　アスクト　　　　　　　　　▶ アスッ＿ト
☞ 破裂音 [k] が脱落する。

❼ getting 　　　　　　　　　ゲッティング　　　　　　　▶ ゲッディ [リ] ン＿
☞ 破裂音 [t] が弾音化。末尾の [g] 音が脱落する。

❽ r and r 　　　　　　　　　アー・アンド・アー　　　　　▶ アーアン＿アー
☞ and の [d] 音が脱落する。

❾ in a critical 　　　　　　イン・ア・クリティカゥ　　　▶ イナクリディ [リ] カゥ
☞ in a は連結。critical の破裂音 [t] が弾音化する。

❿ that is 　　　　　　　　　ザット・イズ　　　　　　　▶ ザッディ [リ] ズ
☞ 連結部で破裂音 [t] が弾音化する。

⓫ to 　　　　　　　　　　　　トゥー　　　　　　　　　▶ ドゥ [ル] ー
☞ 破裂音 [t] が弾音化する。

⓬ But all 　　　　　　　　　バット・オーゥ　　　　　　▶ バッド [ロ] ーゥ
☞ 連結部で破裂音 [t] が弾音化する。

⓭ gutted 　　　　　　　　　ガッティッド　　　　　　　▶ ガッディ [リ] ッド
☞ 破裂音 [t] が弾音化する。

⓮ But a 　　　　　　　　　　バット・ア　　　　　　　　▶ バッダ [ラ]
☞ 連結部で破裂音 [t] が弾音化する。

⓯ instructed 　　　　　　　インストゥラクティッド　　▶ インスチュラクティッド
☞ [tr] の [t] 音は [チュ] のように変化する。

戦争ドラマ　213

Unit 35 医療系ラブコメ
Doctor/Romance Comedy (Grey's Anatomy type)

Stage 1 穴埋めドラマ・リスニング

音声変化に注意してCDでドラマの音声を聴きながら空欄部分を埋めてみよう。CDのナチュラル音声での聴き取りが難しいときは、次のトラックに収録されたスロー音声で聴いてみよう。

● ● ● ● ●

A Are you ① _____ already?

B Is that ② _____ _____ be funny? I just pulled four ③ _____ shifts. I ④ _____ _____ this tired since my residency days.

A ⑤ _____ _____ you look so, so … well, alive at least.

B Such a charmer. What's your excuse? How come you ⑥ _____ _____ play hooky?

A Surgery was postponed. I'm due back here for a consultation ⑦ _____ _____ couple hours.

B Wow, a man of leisure. I wish I had your life.

A You can have my … coffee. Would you like my coffee? I mean, ⑧ _____ _____ buy you a cup of coffee?

B I'm heading straight home. I'm exhausted. And besides, David, your days of 'buying me coffee' are over. How's Sheila these days?

214

A Hey, come on. I ⑨ _____ implying anything. Just, you look so tired, and I just hope that ⑩ _____ _____ _____ can ⑪ _____ _____ get back to what we had, BEFORE we were together. You know, friends?

B Friends is cool. ⑫ _____, David, I DO consider you a friend. Just ⑬ _____ _____ particularly close one. Those, I ⑭ _____ _____ trust.

A Owch. Okay, I deserve that. But can't we ...

B David, no. We can't. I'm going home now. To sleep. By myself. I'm actually ⑮ _____ _____ prefer it that way.

Stage 2 ドラマのシーン解説

日本語訳と、解説を参照しながら、ドラマの内容を確認しよう。そのあとで、Stage1の穴埋めに再チャレンジしてみよう。

A Are you ① **leaving** already?

もう帰るの？

B Is that ② **supposed to** be funny? I just pulled four ③ **straight** shifts. I ④ **haven't been** this tired since my residency days.

それって笑いを取ってるの？ ちょうど、4連続シフトをなんとか終えたところなのよ。研修医時代以来、こんなに疲れたことはないわ。

＊ pull「大変なことをやり遂げる」 residency「研修医の期間」

A ⑤ **And yet** you look so, so ... well, alive at least.

でも、君はとても、とても、その…生存はしてるように見えるよ、少なくとも。

* alive「命があって」

B Such a charmer. What's your excuse? How come you ⑥ **get to** play hooky?

あら、おやさしいのねぇ。で、あなたの口実はなんなの？ どうして、サボっているの？

* charmer「やさしい人；誘惑する人；女たらし」 excuse「口実」 get to ...「…の状態になる」
play hooky「サボる」

A Surgery was postponed. I'm due back here for a consultation ⑦ **in a** couple hours.

手術が延期になったんだ。2時間後に、診察のためにここに戻ることになってるんだ。

* be due back「戻ることになっている」 consultation「診察」

B Wow, a man of leisure. I wish I had your life.

へえ、暇人なのね。私も、あなたの人生が欲しいわ。

* man of leisure「暇な人物」

A You can have my ... coffee. Would you like my coffee? I mean, ⑧ **can I** buy you a cup of coffee?

僕の…コーヒーをあげるよ。僕のコーヒー飲むかい？ あっ、コーヒーを1杯、君におごってもいいかな？

B I'm heading straight home. I'm exhausted. And besides, David, your days of 'buying me coffee' are over. How's Sheila these days?

私はまっすぐ家に帰るつもりなの。ヘトヘトなのよ。それにね、デイヴィッド、あなたが「私にコーヒーをおごってくれる」日々は終わったのよ。最近、シーラはどうしてるの？

Ⓐ Hey, come on. I ⑨ **wasn't** implying anything. Just, you look so tired, and I just hope that ⑩ **you and I** can ⑪ **sort of** get back to what we had, BEFORE we were together. You know, friends?

おい、なに言ってんだよ。僕はなにもほのめかしてなんかいないよ。ただ、君がとても疲れてるようだったし、ただ僕は、君と僕がつき合ってた以前の関係になんとなく戻れたらなと思ってるんだ。あのね、友達かなぁ。

* imply「暗にほのめかす」 get back to ...「…に戻る」

Ⓑ Friends is cool. ⑫ **Actually**, David, I DO consider you a friend. Just ⑬ **not a** particularly close one. Those, I ⑭ **need to** trust.

友達ならいいわよ。実際、私はね、デイヴィッド、あなたのことを友達だと思ってるの。ただ特に親しい友達ってわけじゃないわ。私が頼りにするべき友達ではね。

* cool = okay   trust「頼りにする；信頼する」

Ⓐ Owch. Okay, I deserve that. But can't we …

ありゃりゃ。いいよ。それなら僕にもなれるね。でもさ、ダメなのかな、僕ら…

* deserve ...「…に値する」

Ⓑ David, no. We can't. I'm going home now. To sleep. By myself. I'm actually ⑮ **starting to** prefer it that way.

デイヴィッド、ダメよ。無理なの。私はもう家に帰るんだから。眠りにね。ひとりっきりでよ。実際、そういうのが気に入ってきているのよ。

Stage 3 　英文トランスクリプション

ドラマのシーン全体を英文の原稿で確認しながらCDで耳慣らししよう！　その上で、ドラマ・シーンの音声を聴きながら、まだできていない部分の穴埋めに再チャレンジしよう。

● ● ● ● ● ●

A Are you ① **leaving** already?

B Is that ② **supposed to** be funny? I just pulled four ③ **straight** shifts. I ④ **haven't been** this tired since my residency days.

A ⑤ **And yet** you look so, so ... well, alive at least.

B Such a charmer. What's your excuse? How come you ⑥ **get to** play hooky?

A Surgery was postponed. I'm due back here for a consultation ⑦ **in a** couple hours.

B Wow, a man of leisure. I wish I had your life.

A You can have my ... coffee. Would you like my coffee? I mean, ⑧ **can I** buy you a cup of coffee?

B I'm heading straight home. I'm exhausted. And besides, David, your days of 'buying me coffee' are over. How's Sheila these days?

A Hey, come on. I ⑨ **wasn't** implying anything. Just, you look so tired, and I just hope that ⑩ **you and I** can ⑪ **sort of** get back to what we had, BEFORE we were together. You know, friends?

B Friends is cool. ⑫ **Actually**, David, I DO consider you a friend. Just ⑬ **not a** particularly close one. Those, I ⑭ **need to** trust.

A Owch. Okay, I deserve that. But can't we ...

B David, no. We can't. I'm going home now. To sleep. By myself. I'm actually ⑮ **starting to** prefer it that way.

218

Stage 4 音声変化をチェック

まとめとして、穴埋め部分の音声変化の特徴を**スロー・スピード**と**ナチュラル・スピード**で確認しよう。下記に示したカタカナ表記で音声変化を確認して、もう一度ドラマを聴き直してみよう。発音変化のルールは適宜復習しよう。

❶ **leaving**   リーヴィング   ▶ リーヴィン＿
☞ 末尾の破裂音 [g] が脱落する。

❷ **supposed to**   サポウズド・トゥー   ▶ サポウズッ＿トゥー
☞ supposed の破裂音 [d] が脱落する。

❸ **straight**   ストゥレイト   ▶ スチュレイト
☞ [tr] の [t] 音は [チュ] のように変化する。

❹ **haven't been**   ハヴント・ビーン   ▶ ハヴン＿ビン
☞ haven't 末尾の破裂音 [t] が脱落。been は弱化して [ビン] という発音になる。

❺ **And yet**   アンド・イェット   ▶ アン＿イェッ＿
☞ 両方の単語から末尾の破裂音が脱落する。

❻ **get to**   ゲット・トゥー   ▶ ゲッ＿トゥー
☞ get 末尾の破裂音 [t] が脱落する。

❼ **in a**   イン・ア   ▶ イナ
☞ 2語が連結する。

❽ **can I**   キャン・アイ   ▶ キャナイ
☞ 2語が連結する。

❾ **wasn't**   ワズント   ▶ ワズン＿
☞ 末尾の破裂音 [t] が脱落する。

❿ **you and I**   ユー・アンド・アイ   ▶ ユーアナイ
☞ and 末尾の破裂音 [d] が脱落しつつ、I に連結する。

⓫ **sort of**   ソート・アヴ   ▶ ソーダ [ラ] ヴ
☞ 連結部で破裂音 [t] が弾音化する。

⓬ **Actually**   アクチャリー   ▶ アクシャリー
☞ 破裂音 [t] が脱落する。

⓭ **not a**   ナット・ア   ▶ ナッダ [ラ]
☞ 連結部で破裂音 [t] が弾音化する。

⓮ **need to**   ニード・トゥー   ▶ ニーッ＿トゥー
☞ need 末尾の破裂音 [d] が脱落する。

⓯ **starting to**   スターティング・トゥー   ▶ スターディ [リ] ン＿トゥー
☞ starting の破裂音 [t] が弾音化、末尾の [g] 音は脱落する。

Unit 36 エンタメ業界ドラマ
Entertainment Industry Drama (30 Rock type)

Stage 1 穴埋めドラマ・リスニング

音声変化に注意してCDでドラマの音声を聴きながら空欄部分を埋めてみよう。CDのナチュラル音声での聴き取りが難しいときは、次のトラックに収録されたスロー音声で聴いてみよう。

● ● ● ● ●

A So let me ① _____ _____ straight ... they're gonna put some ② _____-year-old kid in charge of MY department?

B Well, it's not YOUR department anymore. Otherwise THEY ③ _____ do anything of the kind.

A What's that ④ _____ _____ mean? Are you ⑤ _____ _____ tell me that you support their decision?

B Jake, I was the ARCHITECT of 'their' decision. I fought for that 30- year-old 'kid' like he was my own little baby in ⑥ _____ _____ braces. He's 35, by the way.

A But why? How could you do this to me? You just want to humiliate me, ⑦ _____ _____?

B ⑧ _____ _____ has to be ⑨ _____ you, ⑩ _____ _____? Jake, I hate to use a lot of cliches on you, but wake up and smell the coffee. The times, they are a changin'.

A You forgot roses are red, violets are blue. Anyway, you're crazy. I know ⑪ _____ _____ run this department ⑫ _____ than some business school tech geek.

B We were taken over, Jake. We didn't move with the times, we lost ⑬ _____ _____ opportunities, and lo and behold, a younger, smarter company swooped in and ⑭ _____ _____. I can live with that. It's business. You're ⑮ _____ _____ have to too.

Stage 2　ドラマのシーン解説

日本語訳と、解説を参照しながら、ドラマの内容を確認しよう。そのあとで、Stage1の穴埋めに再チャレンジしてみよう。

A So let me ① **get this** straight ... they're gonna put some ② **30-year-old kid** in charge of MY department?

で、これだけははっきりさせておこう…奴ら、俺の部を30歳かそこいらのガキに担当させるつもりなのか？

* in charge of ...「…を担当して」

B Well, it's not YOUR department anymore. Otherwise THEY ③ **couldn't** do anything of the kind.

あのね、もうあなたの部ではないのよ。そうでなければ、彼らにはこんなことできなかったわよ。

🅐 What's that ④ **supposed to** mean? Are you ⑤ **trying to** tell me that you support their decision?

どういうことだ？ 君は奴らの決定を支持すると言おうとしているのか？

* supposed ...「…であるはずの」

🅑 Jake, I was the ARCHITECT of 'their' decision. I fought for that 30-year-old 'kid' like he was my own little baby in ⑥ **need of** braces. He's 35, by the way.

ジェイク、私が彼らの決定を立案したの。私はその30歳のガキのために闘ったの。歯の矯正器具が必要な自分の小っちゃな赤ん坊のためでもあるかのようにね。彼の年齢は35歳だけどね。

* architect「立案者」 braces「歯の矯正具」

🅐 But why? How could you do this to me? You just want to humiliate me, ⑦ **don't you**?

でも、なぜなんだ？ どうして、君は僕にこんな仕打ちができたんだ？ 単に僕を侮辱したいだけなんじゃないのか？

* humiliate「侮辱する」

🅑 ⑧ **It always** has to be ⑨ **about** you, ⑩ **doesn't it**? Jake, I hate to use a lot of cliches on you, but wake up and smell the coffee. The times, they are a changin'.

この世はあなたを中心に回っているんじゃないのよ。あなたのことで、たくさんの決まり文句を使うのはいやなんだけど、目を覚ましてしゃきっとしなさいよ。時代は変わるものなのよ。

* It always has to be about you, doesn't it?「世界はあなたを中心に回っているのではない」直訳すると、「いつも物事はあなたに関係しなくちゃならないんでしょ？」となる。
　hate to ...「…するのを嫌がる」 cliche「決まり文句；常套句」
　The times, they are a changin'.「時代は変わっているのだ」この a には、特別な意味はない。

Ⓐ You forgot roses are red, violets are blue. Anyway, you're crazy. I know ⑪ **how to** run this department ⑫ **better** than some business school tech geek.

「バラは赤く、スミレが青い」っていうフレーズを忘れているよ。とにかく、君はどうかしている。僕はこの部をもっとうまく動かす方法を知っているんだよ、そこいらのビジネス・スクール出の専門用語オタクよりはね。

* roses are red, violets are blue「バラは赤く、スミレは青い」Roses are red, violets are blue. I look like a money, but so do you. (バラは赤く、スミレは青い。私はサルに似てるけど、あんたもね) のようにバカバカしい内容の短い詩をつくるときによく使われる。
  tech geek「専門用語オタク」

Ⓑ We were taken over, Jake. We didn't move with the times, we lost ⑬ **out on** opportunities, and lo and behold, a younger, smarter company swooped in and ⑭ **bought us**. I can live with that. It's business. You're ⑮ **going to** have to too.

うちは買収されたのよ、ジェイク。時代に取り残されて、チャンスを取り損なった、そして驚くなかれ、もっと若くてスマートな会社が突然やってきてうちを買収したの。私はそれでかまわないの。ビジネスなのよ。あなたも、そうしなきゃダメなのよ。

* take over「買収する」 lose out on ...「…を取り損なう」
  lo and behold「驚くなかれ；なんとまあ」 swoop in「突然、入ってくる」
  I can live with that.「私はそれでかまわない」

Stage 3 英文トランスクリプション

ドラマのシーン全体を英文の原稿で確認しながらCDで耳慣らししよう！ その上で、ドラマ・シーンの音声を聴きながら、まだできていない部分の穴埋めに再チャレンジしよう。

• • • • • •

Ⓐ So let me ① **get this** straight ... they're gonna put some ② **30**-year-old kid in charge of MY department?

Ⓑ Well, it's not YOUR department anymore. Otherwise THEY ③ **couldn't** do anything of the kind.

Ⓐ What's that ④ **supposed to** mean? Are you ⑤ **trying to** tell me that you support their decision?

Ⓑ Jake, I was the ARCHITECT of 'their' decision. I fought for that 30-year-old 'kid' like he was my own little baby in ⑥ **need of** braces. He's 35, by the way.

Ⓐ But why? How could you do this to me? You just want to humiliate me, ⑦ **don't you**?

Ⓑ ⑧ **It always** has to be ⑨ **about** you, ⑩ **doesn't it**? Jake, I hate to use a lot of cliches on you, but wake up and smell the coffee. The times, they are a changin'.

Ⓐ You forgot roses are red, violets are blue. Anyway, you're crazy. I know ⑪ **how to** run this department ⑫ **better** than some business school tech geek.

Ⓑ We were taken over, Jake. We didn't move with the times, we lost ⑬ **out on** opportunities, and lo and behold, a younger, smarter company swooped in and ⑭ **bought us**. I can live with that. It's business. You're ⑮ **going to** have to too.

Stage 4 音声変化をチェック

まとめとして、穴埋め部分の音声変化の特徴を**スロー・スピード**と**ナチュラル・スピード**で確認しよう。下記に示したカタカナ表記で音声変化を確認して、もう一度ドラマを聴き直してみよう。発音変化のルールは適宜復習しよう。

❶ **get this** ゲット・ズィス ▶ ゲッ__ズィス
☞ get の破裂音 [t] が脱落する。

❷ **30** サーティー ▶ サーディ [リ] ー
☞ 破裂音 [t] が弾音化する。

❸ **couldn't** クドゥント ▶ クンン__
☞ [dn] の [d] 音が声門閉鎖音化する。末尾の [t] 音は脱落。

❹ **supposed to** サポウズド・トゥー ▶ サポウスッ__トゥー
☞ supposed の [z] 音が [s] 音に変化、末尾の [d] 音は脱落する。

❺ **trying to** トゥライイング・トゥー ▶ チュライヌー
☞ trying 先頭の [tr] では、[t] 音が [チュ] のように変化する。trying 末尾の [g] 音が脱落しつつ、弱化した to [ə/u] に連結する。

❻ **need of** ニード・アヴ ▶ ニーダ [ラ] ヴ
☞ 2語が連結。連結部で [d] 音が弾音化する場合もある。

❼ **don't you** ドゥント・ユー ▶ ドン__ユー
☞ don't は弱化し、末尾の破裂音 [t] 音が脱落する。

❽ **It always** イット・オーゥウェイズ ▶ イッド [ロ] ーゥウェイズ
☞ 連結部で [t] 音が弾音化する。

❾ **about** アバウト ▶ アバウッ__
☞ 末尾の破裂音 [t] が脱落する。

❿ **doesn't it** ダズント・イット ▶ ダズニッ__
☞ doesn't 末尾の破裂音 [t] が脱落しつつ、it に連結する。it 末尾の破裂音 [t] が脱落する。

⓫ **how to** ハウ・トゥー ▶ ハウドゥ [ル]
☞ 弱化した to [tə/tu] の [t] 音が弾音化する。

⓬ **better** ベター ▶ ベダ [ラ] ー
☞ 破裂音 [t] が弾音化する。

⓭ **out on** アウト・オン ▶ アウド [ロ] ン
☞ 連結部で [t] 音が弾音化する。

⓮ **bought us** ボート・アス ▶ ボーダ [ラ] ス
☞ 連結部で [t] 音が弾音化する。

⓯ **going to** ゴウイング・トゥー ▶ ゴウイン__ドゥ [ル] ー
☞ going 末尾の [g] 音が脱落。to の破裂音 [t] が弾音化する。

エンタメ業界ドラマ

Unit 37 法律ドラマ
Legal Drama (Law & Order type)

Stage 1 穴埋めドラマ・リスニング

音声変化に注意してCDでドラマの音声を聴きながら空欄部分を埋めてみよう。CDのナチュラル音声での聴き取りが難しいときは、次のトラックに収録されたスロー音声で聴いてみよう。

● ● ● ● ●

A Mr. Hogan, you claim ① _____ the last time you saw your ex-wife was three nights before her murder, ② _____ _____ _____ at her home, correct?

B Yes. We ③ _____ _____ fight, and I left early. ④ _____ _____ no plans to ⑤ _____ _____ after that.

A Oh, yes, indeed you ⑥ _____ _____ fight. Other people attending the party clearly heard you ⑦ _____ to kill her.

B I was very angry! Ask anyone who was there. ⑧ _____ _____ the ⑨ _____ _____ thing people say when they are really angry; that's all.

A ⑩ _____ _____, three days later, she WAS killed. Mr. Hogan, surely you can understand how you come to be here on this stand ⑪ _____ _____.

B I didn't kill Val! It's true that I was often angry with her. That's why our marriage failed. ⑫ _____ _____ was never violent ⑬ _____ _____.

226

A True, she never filed any reports of domestic violence. But you have been violent in the past, with others. We have records of bar fights, incidents with paparazzi.

B Always men! I ⑭ _____ _____ women! I never hurt Val!

A That's your claim, Mr. Hogan. ⑮ _____ your record clearly shows violent outbursts when someone has wronged you. And you felt wronged by your ex-wife.

Stage 2 ドラマのシーン解説

日本語訳と、解説を参照しながら、ドラマの内容を確認しよう。そのあとで、Stage1の穴埋めに再チャレンジしてみよう。

A Mr. Hogan, you claim ① **that** the last time you saw your ex-wife was three nights before her murder, ② **at a party** at her home, correct?

ホーガンさん、あなたは、離婚した奥さんと会ったのは、彼女の殺害の3晩前が最後だと主張していますね。彼女の家のパーティーで。そのとおりですか？

* ex-wife「別れた妻」

B Yes. We ③ **had a** fight, and I left early. ④ **I had** no plans to ⑤ **contact her** after that.

ええ。僕らはケンカしたので、私は早めに帰りました。そのあと、彼女に会う予定はありませんでしたよ。

＊ fight「ケンカ；口論」

A Oh, yes, indeed you ⑥ **had a** fight. Other people attending the party clearly heard you ⑦ **threaten** to kill her.

ええ、そうですね、実際あなたがたはケンカしました。パーティーに出席していたほかの人たちが、あなたが彼女を殺すと脅したのをはっきりと耳にしていました。

＊ threaten「脅す」

B I was very angry! Ask anyone who was there. ⑧ **It was** the ⑨ **kind of** thing people say when they are really angry; that's all.

とても頭にきていたんです！ その場にいた人のだれにでも聞いてください。言わば、ものすごく頭にきた人間が言う類いのことですし、それだけだったんです。

＊ that's all「それがすべてだ」

A ⑩ **And yet**, three days later, she WAS killed. Mr. Hogan, surely you can understand how you come to be here on this stand ⑪ **right now**.

ところが、その3日後に彼女は殺害された。ホーガンさん、あなたが、どうしていまこの証言台に立たされることになったのかは、はっきり理解できますね。

＊ And yet, ...「どころが…；なおかつ…；さりながら…」 stand「証言台；証人席」

B I didn't kill Val! It's true that I was often angry with her. That's why our marriage failed. ⑫ **But I** was never violent ⑬ **with her**.

私はヴァルを殺してはいない！ よく彼女に腹を立てていたのは確かだ。それが原因で、僕らの結婚生活は壊れたんですよ。でも、彼女に暴力を振るったことは一度もないんだ。

＊ violent「暴力的な」

Ⓐ True, she never filed any reports of domestic violence. But you have been violent in the past, with others. We have records of bar fights, incidents with paparazzi.

そうですね。彼女はいかなる DV の被害届も出してはいません。でも、あなたは過去、ほかの人たちに暴力的だったことがありますね。バーでのケンカやパパラッチとの暴力事件の前科があります。

＊ file a report「被害届を出す」　domestic violence「家庭内暴力」　record「前科；記録」
　incident「暴力事件」　paparazzi ＝ paparazzo の複数形「有名人を追い回すカメラマン」

Ⓑ Always men! I ⑭ **don't hurt** women! I never hurt Val!

いつも相手は男性だ！ 私は女性を傷つけたりはしない！ ヴァルを傷つけたことは一度もないんだ！

Ⓐ That's your claim, Mr. Hogan. ⑮ **But** your record clearly shows violent outbursts when someone has wronged you. And you felt wronged by your ex-wife.

ホーガンさん、それはあなたの言い分ですね。しかし、あなたの前科から、だれかがあなたを中傷したとき、あなたが怒りを暴力的に爆発させることは明らかです。そして、あなたは、あなたの前妻に中傷されたと感じたのです。

＊ outburst「(怒りなどの) 爆発」　wrong「中傷する」

Stage 3 英文トランスクリプション

ドラマのシーン全体を英文の原稿で確認しながらCDで耳慣らししよう！ その上で、ドラマ・シーンの音声を聴きながら、まだできていない部分の穴埋めに再チャレンジしよう。

● ● ● ● ● ●

A Mr. Hogan, you claim ① **that** the last time you saw your ex-wife was three nights before her murder, ② **at a party** at her home, correct?

B Yes. We ③ **had a** fight, and I left early. ④ **I had** no plans to ⑤ **contact her** after that.

A Oh, yes, indeed you ⑥ **had a** fight. Other people attending the party clearly heard you ⑦ **threaten** to kill her.

B I was very angry! Ask anyone who was there. ⑧ **It was** the ⑨ **kind of** thing people say when they are really angry; that's all.

A ⑩ **And yet**, three days later, she WAS killed. Mr. Hogan, surely you can understand how you come to be here on this stand ⑪ **right now**.

B I didn't kill Val! It's true that I was often angry with her. That's why our marriage failed. ⑫ **But I** was never violent ⑬ **with her**.

A True, she never filed any reports of domestic violence. But you have been violent in the past, with others. We have records of bar fights, incidents with paparazzi.

B Always men! I ⑭ **don't hurt** women! I never hurt Val!

A That's your claim, Mr. Hogan. ⑮ **But** your record clearly shows violent outbursts when someone has wronged you. And you felt wronged by your ex-wife.

Stage 4 音声変化をチェック

CD 2-54

まとめとして、穴埋め部分の音声変化の特徴を**スロー・スピード**と**ナチュラル・スピード**で確認しよう。下記に示したカタカナ表記で音声変化を確認して、もう一度ドラマを聴き直してみよう。発音変化のルールは適宜復習しよう。

❶ that ザット ▶ ザッ＿
☞ 末尾の破裂音 [t] が脱落する。

❷ at a party アット・ア・パーティー ▶ アッダ [ラ] パーディ [リ] ー
☞ at a の連結部と party で破裂音 [t] が弾音化する。

❸ had a ハッド・ア ▶ ハッダ [ラ]
☞ 連結部で [d] 音が弾音化する。

❹ I had アイ・ハッド ▶ アイ＿ド
☞ had が弱化して [d] の音だけになる。

❺ contact her コンタクト・ハー ▶ コンタクター
☞ contact が弱化した her [ər] に連結する。

❻ had a ハッド・ア ▶ ハッダ [ラ]
☞ ❸ と同様の変化が生じる。

❼ threaten スレトゥン ▶ スレんン
☞ [tn] の [t] 音が声門閉鎖音化する。

❽ It was イット・ワズ ▶ イッ＿ワズ
☞ it の破裂音 [t] が脱落する。

❾ kind of カインド・アヴ ▶ カインダッ＿
☞ 2語が連結。of 末尾の [v] 音も脱落しやすい。

❿ And yet アンド・イェット ▶ アン＿イェッ＿
☞ 2語それぞれの末尾の破裂音が脱落する。

⓫ right now ライト・ナウ ▶ ライッ＿ナウ
☞ right 末尾の破裂音 [t] が脱落する。

⓬ But I バット・アイ ▶ バッダ [ラ] イ
☞ 連結部で [t] 音が弾音化する。

⓭ with her ウィズ・ハー ▶ ウィザー
☞ with が弱化した her [ər] に連結する。

⓮ don't hurt ドウント・フート ▶ ドン＿フー (ト)
☞ 弱化した don't 末尾の [t] 音や hurt 末尾の [t] 音が脱落する。

⓯ But バット ▶ バッ＿
☞ 末尾の破裂音 [t] が脱落する。

法律ドラマ 231

■ 著者略歴

長尾 和夫 (Kazuo Nagao)
福岡県出身。南雲堂出版、アスク講談社、NOVA などで、大学英語教科書や語学系書籍・CD-ROM・Web サイトなどの編集・制作・執筆に携わる。現在、語学書籍の出版プロデュース・執筆・編集・翻訳などを行うアルファ・プラス・カフェ(www.alphapluscafe.com) を主宰。『絶対「英語の耳」になる!』シリーズ全15点 (三修社)、『日常生活を英語でドンドン説明してみよう』(アスク出版)、『英会話 見たまま練習帳』(DHC)、『ビジネス英会話 高速変換トレーニング』(アルク)、『英語で自分をアピールできますか?』『英語でケンカができますか?』(角川グループパブリッシング)、『書き込み式・英語で自分を説明できる本』(日本経済新聞出版社)、『ネイティブ英語がこう聞こえたら、この英語だ!』(主婦の友社) ほか、著訳書・編書は250点を超える。『English Journal』(アルク)、『CNN English Express』(朝日出版社) など、雑誌媒体への寄稿も行っている。

アンディ・バーガー (Andy Boerger)
米国出身。オハイオ州立大学で BFA を取得。横浜国立大学講師。サイマルアカデミー CTC (Simul Academy Corporate Training Center)、アルク、タイムライフなどでの英会話講師経験を活かし、A+Café (アルファ・プラス・カフェ) の主要メンバーとして、多岐にわたる語学書籍の執筆に活躍中。主著に、『絶対「英語の口」になる! 中学英語で基礎から鍛えるシャドーイング大特訓50』『絶対「英語の耳」になる! リスニング50のルール』(三修社)、『聴こえる!話せる!ネイティヴ英語発音の法則』『ネイティブみたいに主張する! 激論 English』(DHC)、『英文メールにとにかく 100 語で書いてみる』(すばる舎)、『英語で返事ができますか?』(角川グループパブリッシング)、『ビジネスパワー英語入門 243』(PHP 研究所) などがある。

絶対『英語の耳』になる!
TVドラマ・シーンで鍛える!
ネイティヴ英語リスニング37

2015年5月10日 第1刷発行

著　者	長尾和夫　アンディ・バーガー
発行者	前田俊秀
発行所	株式会社三修社

〒 150-0001　東京都渋谷区神宮前 2-2-22
TEL 03-3405-4511　FAX 03-3405-4522
振替 00190-9-72758
http://www.sanshusha.co.jp/
編集担当　北村英治

印刷・製本　壮光舎印刷株式会社

©2015 A+Café　Printed in Japan
ISBN978-4-384-04639-7 C2082

®〈日本複製権センター委託出版物〉
本書を無断で複写複製 (コピー) することは、著作権法上の例外を除き、禁じられています。
本書をコピーされる場合は、事前に日本複製権センター (JRRC) の許諾を受けてください。
JRRC〈http://www.jrrc.or.jp e-mail：info@jrrc.or.jp　電話：03-3401-2382〉